MW01702841

HOW I GOT MY KICKS

Ann Murphy

INFINITY
PUBLISHING

All rights reserved. No part of this book shall be reproduced or transmitted in any form or by any means, electronic, mechanical, magnetic, photographic including photocopying, recording or by any information storage and retrieval system, without prior written permission of the publisher. No patent liability is assumed with respect to the use of the information contained herein. Although every precaution has been taken in the preparation of this book, the publisher and author assume no responsibility for errors or omissions. Neither is any liability assumed for damages resulting from the use of the information contained herein.

Copyright © 2015 by Ann Murphy

ISBN 978-0-7414-9972-1 Hardcover
ISBN 978-1-4958-0172-3 Softcover

Published April 2015

INFINITY PUBLISHING
1094 New DeHaven Street, Suite 100
West Conshohocken, PA 19428-2713
Toll-free (877) BUY BOOK
Local Phone (610) 941-9999
Fax (610) 941-9959
Info@buybooksontheweb.com
www.buybooksontheweb.com

Dedication

This book is dedicated
to the loving memory of my dear,
sweet actor, Lou Ruggiero.

RUSSELL MARKERT

Every Rockette, past and present, owes her Rockettesmanship to the man pictured above—Russell Markert. Inspired by seeing the John Tiller girls of England in the 1922 production of The Ziegfield Follies, Russell had an idea and a vision. He dreamed of a line of American girls. He wanted them tall, with long legs, and the ability to tap and kick precisely in unison with one another.

His vision achieved reality in 1925 as the sixteen "Missouri Rockets" made their dancing debut in St. Louis. By the late 1920s there were forty-six of them at the Roxy Theatre and they were then known as "The Roxyettes."

In 1932 they moved a block away, to Radio City Music Hall, where they opened on December 27th. Later the name was changed to "The Rockettes" as it remains today.

Fred Astaireian in physique and dance style, Russell was also a father figure to the girls. He was dashing, he was dapper, and always a gentleman who had the uncanny ability of remembering a girl's name even if he had only met her once.

His unique routines remain in the dance memories of many a Rockette over the ages. From the cowboy, to the sailor, to Shakin' the Blues, to Cindy Lou, to Beauty and the Beat, Fiddle Faddle, and, of course, the Wooden Soldier and so many others–they were all classics. And so was Russell–a class act.

TABLE OF CONTENTS

PREFACE

The one thing I disliked the most about my career was the continuous dressing and undressing I did throughout the course of a day. I got up in the morning and put on my bathrobe. I had breakfast, did the dishes, made my bed, and took off my robe and put on my clothes. I went to work and took off my clothes and put on my robe. I put on my makeup and took off my robe. I put on my costume (or costumes, as the show might call for several costumes–don't forget those quick changes), did the show and went back to the dressing room, took off my costume, and put on my robe. I cooled off, took off my robe and put on my street clothes. And so it went, ad infinitum, throughout the day and into the night. No wonder I sleep in the buff! All kicking aside, the dressing and undressing will kill you.

As the wonderfully talented Elaine Stritch, in her glorious show "Elaine Stritch At Liberty" said of a prostitute who was complaining of her line of work, "It's not about the work; it's the stairs. Think about it."

Chapter 1

SHY BUTTERFLY TAKES OFF

The month was March. The day was cold and rainy. The setting was Boston's Logan Airport, where my mother, her friend and I were awaiting a plane that was to take extremely shy and introverted junior in high school me to New York. If mom was nervous, she never let on that she was. After all, her little darling was flying to New York "in a plane?" (to quote my astonishingly perplexed father when he first heard of the shenanigans) "to audition for a, er, uh, er, a "road show." Mom's response to dad's "in a plane?" "Well, Bill, she's not going to use her arms."

As a kid, I'd always said I'd never set foot on an airplane. Well, there I was eating my words. Nothing could stop me now–no rain, no wind, no money–hmm–nothing. I was going to get to New York to make that audition, no matter what!

The three of us had been standing in the American Airlines waiting room for quite some time when my mother's friend, Charlie, spotted an old friend of his. Andy was his name. The two men shook hands and exchanged greetings. After discovering that Andy was New York bound, too, Charlie asked him if he'd "sort of keep an eye on the little girl standing over there." Andy's eyes wandered across the room and stopped when he eyed a luscious looking blond. Obviously, a showgirl, I thought. "Oh Mom," I said, "he doesn't like me; he's looking at her." "No, no," Charlie laughed, "not the blond, the little brunette right over there."

"Oh, sure Charlie," came the reply, "Be glad to." I wondered if that blond was auditioning for the same show I was.

A few weeks prior to this airport scene, I had been at dancing school one Saturday afternoon, when my dance teacher, Geraldine Paré, gave me a booklet to look over while I was waiting to go into the studio to take my lesson. The booklet was called "Dancer's Notebook" and was published by Selva Dance Company, a dance shoe manufacturer in New York. My dance teacher had told me to pay particular attention to one very special paragraph. While she went back into the studio to finish up a lesson, I read it through carefully.

It seemed that Mr. Russell Markert, creator and director of the Radio City Music Hall Rockettes, was looking for girls who wanted to go out on a road show, which would tour the United States and Canada. The show was scheduled to run for twelve weeks. The requirements were good tap, jazz and ballet background, and high, limber kicks, which were typical of Rockette requirements.

To be precise, the then requirements for becoming a Rockette were a good sense of rhythm and musicality. The basic tap foundation would include single, double, and triple time steps, traveling time steps, cramp roll time steps, various tap combinations, and, of course, those eye high kicks, and sometimes higher.

An audition would also include some ballet combinations. To determine balance, a girl might be asked to do a series of piqué and chainé turns.

Oh, if only I could do this, I thought. My mother had been after me for weeks to please get a part-time job. After all, I was a junior in high school and like most teenagers of low and middle income families, I needed a job.

My dance teacher came out of the studio. As she was wiping her hair back from her face, she asked, "Well, what do you think?"

"Do you think I could do it?"

"Sure you could," she replied. "Why don't you at least try? That, in itself, will be an experience. I would if I were you."

That day I left the studio on cloud nine.

When my mother got home from work that evening, I announced that I was taking off from school Monday and flying to New York first thing in the morning to audition for a road show.

"Oh, no you're not, young lady" is what I thought I'd be hearing from my mom. I even had an argument ready. She had told me to get a job, but she didn't say where. Now, at least, I was trying. Besides, she was in show business when she was younger. Well, to my amazement, she didn't give me any argument.

Ever since I first started to study dancing at the age of three, I wanted to be a dancer. And ever since I was in the eighth grade, I deposited money into a savings account, which I had opened with the idea that some day I'd use it to go to New York. I had $2.50; I don't remember why I had it, but that's what I used to open my account. (Those were the days; now, unfortunately, one needs considerably more to open an account).

My girlfriend, Diane Brown, and I got permission from Eastern Junior High School principal Lewis Thistle to leave the school grounds during lunch hour so I could go the Lynn Institution For Savings and deposit my $2.50. Those were the days of real bankers' hours, when banks were not open before I went to school at 8:30 a.m. and when I got out of school at 2:30 p.m. Banking hours were from 9:00 a.m. to 2:00 p.m.

Twice a year I deposited money into my account-Christmas and my birthday. Mighty slow savings, but I had enough to fly down to New York to make the audition. Latently, I think I had secretly hoped my mother would give me the money. But mom wisely asked me "Isn't that the New York fund?"

"Yeah, it's the New York fund," I acceptingly responded.

Very calmly mom said, "Well, let's walk over to your father's and discuss this with him."

"Bill, Ann's taking off from school Monday and flying down to New York to audition for a road show."

My dad's astonishingly perplexed eyebrows rose toward the ceiling as he asked that famous remark, "In a plane?"

Mom quipped, "Well, she's not going to use her arms."

The conversation was a little heavy, but not too bad. Although Dad did say, "I don't want her running around with a lot of show people." However, finally he reluctantly agreed. "Well, maybe you should give it a try."

I've often wondered if my parents hadn't been divorced, if the outcome would have been different.

And thus, Monday morning finally arrived, and after kissing my mother and Charlie good-bye, and listening to several of my mother's "Be carefuls," trembling with fear but definitely determined, I boarded the plane.

I was on my way!

SHY BUTTERFLY REALLY TAKES OFF

"Good morning, ladies and gentlemen. I'd like to welcome you aboard American Airlines Jet Propelled Electra." And, as we were taxiing down the runway, accelerating, vibrating, and bracing for that shaky take-off, she continued, "On behalf of Captain Tyrell and the crew and myself, we'd like to wish you a pleasant flight. Please observe the no smoking signs and fasten your seat belts. Our destination is New York LaGuardia Airport. Our cruising altitude will be 20,000 feet." And when we got up there—up there in the clouds—bumping and tossing about, this shy, quiet little mouse nervously and sickly reached for one of those little white bags at the back of the seat in front of me.

Those were not the early days of aviation, but it wasn't exactly the days of the Boeing 707, DC10 or wide body 1011, either. It was a jet propeller job.

We might have been on a Jet Propelled Electra, but the flight attendant might as well have been Bette Davis, alias Margo Channing, and said, "Fasten your seat belts; it's going to be a bumpy ride."

Flight sophisticate Andy must have gotten quite a kick out of the sickly fledgling, but he was kind enough to taxi me into the heart of the city. His office was on Fifth Avenue, the International Building, and the Radio City Music Hall building, where my audition was to be held, was right behind it. As we got out of the cab on that rainy day, looking up at those grey buildings, I thought I almost hadn't left Boston. Then I remembered all that time in the air. No, we weren't in Scully Square anymore.

I thanked Andy and, since I had a couple of hours to kill before my audition, I quickly set out for the street of my dreams. The street they talked about, wrote about, sang songs about, and made movies about.

"Excuse me, officer, could you tell me where the street is where all the lights are bright and shining?"

"Hmm? Oh, oh, ah, you mean Broadway." He pointed West and said, "It's two blocks over that way."

So, I tripped over to the light fantastic, saw the glitter, saw the glamour, saw the glum, saw snarling traffic, beautiful, beautiful girls, construction workers and, oh yes, cab drivers who swore like bastards. My sixteen year old brown eyes nearly popped out of my head. Seeing Broadway for the first time was one of the biggest disappointments in my life. I did not expect to see a Nedicks or a Ripley's Believe It Or Not on Broadway. Hell, we had that in Revere Beach. But what I had to realize was that the ideas in my head about Broadway were put there by movies made in Hollywood. Glamorous Ginger Rogers and Fred Astaire danced amid so much elegance and chic. I mean, Nedicks was not exactly "Puttin' on the Ritz." To paraphrase the words from a song in "A Chorus Line:" "Everything was beautiful at the ballet." Everything was beautiful at the movies.

I quickly made my way back to the Music Hall, checked in with the stage doorman, and elevated up to the seventh floor rehearsal hall where I cramp roll time-stepped and eye-high kicked my way through the audition.

Breathlessly, I went back to report to Andy, who took me to lunch at 21 Club. I flew back to Boston later that afternoon and spent the rest of the evening not quite believing what I had done that day.

Anyway, the next few weeks were agonizingly anticipatory, but at last the letter arrived stating that I had passed the audition and was to report for rehearsal on May 12th.

For six weeks we rehearsed in New York's Metropolitan Opera Studios on West 56th Street prior to our opening in Minot, North Dakota. My mother gave me one hundred dollars to last me for six weeks. Of course, this was pre-Great Society days, but not that pre! That certainly was a long S-T-R-E-T-C-H on one hundred dollars.

That first six weeks in the "big city" could easily have been the last six weeks in the big city for the dancing eager little beaver who had grown up in little old Lynn, Massachusetts under the auspices of a Quaker mother and a Catholic father. Why, in less than three days my big brown eyes had their first glimpse of drunks in doorways, poor people, really poor people, glamorous, glamorous girls, homosexuals, and those cabbies. Wow! I was learning lots about this wacky world and how it turns.

There were two auditions and two round trip plane trips before my semi-final move to New York. By my second flight, I was practically a veteran.

My semi-final move came when the "Y'all come" call came from Russell Markert. It seems we were to have a three day trial period to see if we could keep up the pace of a typical chorine (chorus girl)–work long hours, pick up dance steps, and kick "eye high." "Eye high" pronounced with a slightly southern accent is a Russell Markert term, simply meaning the ability to kick at one's own eye level.

I boarded the New York bound train in Boston. We made the usual stops–Back Bay, Route 128 and Providence, Rhode Island. Ah yes, Providence, where I met my intended roommate Barbara Katz. (We had originally met at the second audition). She was between years in college and trying to decide between the collegiate life and the life of show biz. Well, this was a good way to find out–a twelve week tour.

I remember her parents standing on the platform kissing their girl good-bye and giving her their "Be carefuls." It still tickles my memory when I think of her mother peering through the train window, spotting me, shaking her head negatively and giving me that "you couldn't be going to be my daughter's roommate; you're only twelve years old" look.

I must have looked pretty young and scared, and mousy or unworldly or something, for Barbara, my roommate to-be, and I hadn't been sitting together ten minutes when she told me I should change my hair style. "Why don't you do something with your hair?" she questioned. (My brown hair was styled in a pixie cut.) Hmm. These college women! One year in college and they think they're women of the world. Needless to say, our rapport, and I don't know if we had any, got off to a rough start. Years later, actually decades later, Barbara and I met up again in California and she was just as charming as can be. About the only thing that Barbara and I did agree upon was that no matter what happened during that three day trial period, whether we came out of the wash sparkling or went crying home to Mama, we would go see the Broadway show "West Side Story."

Barbara and I shared a room at the YWCA Laura Spellman Residence on 8th Avenue and 50th Street, where we each paid $4.28 per night. That included breakfast and dinner. However, we were rarely there for dinner, as our rehearsals ran into the Y's dinner hour. So, I had a lot of 15-cent macaroni and cheese dinners from the automat.

One day I was lunching in the automat and I must have looked hungry, as a lady slipped a quarter under my dish exclaiming "I just came from The Arthur Godfrey Show and I want you to help me celebrate." I only made 15 cents on the deal, though, as on the way home to the Y, a young man asked me for a dime, so I gave it to him.

Another meal I remember, I went out to lunch with a bunch of the girls and they all ordered hamburgers and Cokes but, watching my money, I ordered a banana and a glass of milk. That $100 had to last me six weeks. The waiter asked me "Do you want the banana in the milk or do you want them separately?" Embarrassed, I whispered "Separately, please." Those hamburgers sure looked good.

Our days were long and grueling. We usually began at 9:00 or 10:00 a.m. and went through to 6:00 p.m., with an hour off for lunch. We had a lot of learning and tapping and kicking to do. There was a smashing opening number where we wore red, white, and blue costumes. It was to Cole Porter's "Another Opening, Another Show" from "Kiss Me Kate." There were six boy dancers and 24 girl dancers, and one swing girl who went on at a moment's notice if one of the girls was out. With the blue group, consisting of eight girls and two boys coming out first, then the white, I was in the last, the red group. Also, a quartet of two men and two women provided the singing accompaniment. And, we were dancing to a live orchestra, some members of which we picked up in each town we played.

Our second number was a Caribbean-style ditty, "Romanza del Caribe" with some steps that Russell said were authentically African. It was a cute little number and fun to do. The third routine was a stunning dance, which I repeated years later with the Rockettes. We wore bright orange fringe slinky skirts with a slit up the side. Sizzling and sexy, it was a hot one to "Shakin' The Blues Away."

Barbara and I would practice in the room at night. Quiet and shy, I asked Barbara if this routine was suggestive. "Oh, it's very suggestive," she said. With the passing of a few years, I had more maturity and was able to put more of my heart, soul and moxie into the bumps and grinds when I did the routine with the Rockettes.

Our finale was all in gold, and large round flat hats spelled out T-H-A-N-K Y-O-U-G-O-O-D N-I-G-H-T in hot pink letters as we did our final bow.

Between those dance numbers we had a female lead singer (actually, she was the Producer's wife, Diane Duncan, but she was very good); a male lead singer, Dan Resin, who later on made a successful career of doing TV commercials; the Julindas, a family acrobatic act, a husband, wife and their three daughters, the youngest of which used to balance her dad on her knees as she was lying on her back. It was very impressive; the child was only three years old. We had a trapeze act that worked the skyway flying and dangling from a helicopter; a tight wire act, Frank & Dolores Evers; the Baraccini Chimps; and the U. S. International Diving Champions featuring a high diver from Mexico, Raol Garcia Ravol.

After three or four weeks of spending $56 each a week to stay at the Y, Barbara and I decided to move to the famous—or infamous—hotel for show people, "The Belvedere Hotel" on West 48th Street. We cut down on expenses by sharing a huge room with two other girls.

Speaking of cutting expenses, my money was running low. I had noticed when Barbara and I went to see "West Side Story" the theatre had usherettes. So, I decided to try to get a job as an usherette. Well, I did, and my first job as one was working at the Lunt-Fontaine Theatre, where I got to watch Alfred Lunt and Lynn Fontaine perform "The Visit" every night–and get paid for it! I couldn't wait to get people seated so I could sit on the balcony stairs and watch these two magnificent actors. The job also got me out of the hotel room, where there would often be a late night party—not my cup of tea. I was very serious. Young, but serious.

Since I was so young, my mother was severely criticized by her peers, with many of them asking "What if she gets pregnant?" I loved my mother's answer. "I'll help her take care of the baby," mom said.

One day I also worked a matinee at the Rivoli movie house. I was up in the balcony and never quite sure where to seat people as there were both odd and even numbers on the seats. One man came in, showed me his ticket and as I studied it and was thinking, thinking, thinking where to place him he said, "Eenie, meeny, miny, mo; up to the balcony I must go." Often I had people seated in the wrong seats and there was a lot of rearranging to do.

At last the weeks of hoofing, kicking, automat eating and putting people in the wrong theatre seats came to an end. As luck would have it, our tour bus was picking up the troupe right in front of our hotel. We had three days to get to our opening date in Minot, North Dakota. On our way to Minot on a Sunday morning we stopped at a luncheonette in Minnesota, where this one poor girl was working all alone. She shuddered and sighed as the busload of singers and dancers piled into the place. Exasperated she announced, "I told the boss not to leave me alone; all right, make your own ice cream sodas." Whipped cream was flying and ice cream was all over the place.

In Minot we performed in a gymnasium with a very slippery floor. The dancers were aghast and petrified. Russell cautioned, "If you fall down, get up with a smile." Many did. It was extremely slippery. Russell and assistant choreographer, Emily Sherman, had flown out to Minot to get the show up and running.

There were twin hotels in Minot–The Clarence Parker Hotel and The Leland Parker Hotel. Behind one of them was a garden where they grew their own fruit and vegetables. They had a wonderful 99-cent luncheon of fresh fruit salad. Decades later I took my husband Tom there, and I had all of Minot reminiscing about that 99-cent fruit salad. "Yes, that was a wonderful lunch" was the echo of the town.

Our next five gigs were in Canada, where we stayed in private residences. Brandon, Manitoba was our first Canadian stop and then on to Calgary, Alberta for the Calgary Stampede week. The show was billed as The International Spectacular of 1958, produced by Jim Hetzer's Theatrical Agency out of Huntington, West Virginia and we played State and Agricultural Industrial fairs. I don't know how I managed it, but I got out of my junior year in high school six weeks early, and returned for my senior year three weeks late. However, the International Spectacular was an education unto itself. I was seeing my country and another one, and being paid $90 a week, which in those days was pretty good money for a sixteen year old.

With chuck-wagon races, Brahma bulls, a circus and a midway, including a stripper called Mitzi of the Midway, the Calgary Stampede were very exciting.

One night after the show, my landlady and her husband, who had come to see the show, took me to a coffee shop, which was packed. A man and his wife were sitting in an exceptionally large booth and motioned for us to join them. My landlady happened to mention that I was "one of the dancing girls at the fair." Well, that got them. All of a sudden there was an interest. "Where you from?" asked the man. "Boston." "Oh, beans–ever rode a horse before?" he asked. Just that day I had been telling Sally, the wardrobe mistress, how I would like to go horseback riding.

So, I was instructed to report very early the next morning to Jim Todd, Barn 17. I felt very western in my jeans and my F.W. Woolworth cowgirl hat as I peeked into the barn. Unshaven men were scattered around the barn, along with a few empty whiskey bottles. Mr. Todd whisked me out of there quickly and told me to come back the next day. Along with the other cowboys, Todd was one of the men who, on horseback, makes sure that the cowboy riding the bucking bronco gets back into the corral safely after being bucked off the horse or bull.

I was leaning over a corral, admiring some horses when all of a sudden a little stranger started talking to me. He was a cute little boy who claimed he was 13; I'd say closer to 10. He reminded me of my little brother Billy, whom I missed dearly. This young wanna-be teenager won my heart when he looked up at me with his big blue eyes and sighed, "I've got the hat, I've got the shirt, I've got the pants, I've got the boots, but I ain't got the horse."

Oh, you poor little deprived boy, I thought and then asked "How would you like to come to the circus with me?" He said that he would. I had a pass that entitled me and a guest to any event on the fairgrounds.

It wasn't Ringling Brothers, but it was a pretty darn good little circus. We sat in the balcony and had cotton candy and Cokes. All of a sudden, I felt a little arm around me and his other hand holding my hand. I sat there stunned, trying to figure out what to do and thinking "you miserable chorus girl out seducing this young boy." Hell, I was only 16 going on 12, and he was 10 going on 30.

We exited the circus and I brought him back to our dressing room (anything to get out of the balcony) to meet our wardrobe people. Sally's comment was "Well, you pick 'em young, don't you Murphy?" It's all right; years later I made up for it when I was attracted to older men.

The next day, Jim Todd took me horseback riding around the rodeo ring. My little friend was watching from the sidelines. After our trek, Todd asked me "Do you think he'd like to ride around, too?" "Yeah, I think he would," I said. So, the horseless would-be teenager got to ride around one of the biggest rodeos in the world.

When the bus left Calgary for Edmonton, my little boyfriend was standing by the curb and sadly waved good-bye.

A civic group in Edmonton took our whole company on a tour of the magnificent state-of-the-art Alberta Jubilee Auditorium. Its identical twin theatre was located in Calgary. We did not see the theatre in Calgary, but we certainly admired its twin sister, which could house opera, symphonies, stage productions, movies, art displays, etc.

In Saskatoon, Saskatchewan I stayed with a delightful little, pert old lady who kept a perfect garden and used to wear those old-fashioned silver metal curlers in her hair. Nanny Green was a fascinating lady and she told me that she had survived the Titanic disaster.

After Regina we went back to the States, where we had a week's respite in Clear Lake, Iowa. (Upon entering the United States, everyone on the bus went into song, singing "My Country 'Tis of Thee," which we'd heard every night in Canada pre-show, only the lyrics were "God Save the Queen.") Then it was onto Cedar Rapids, Iowa, Meredith Wilson country.

In Huntington, West Virginia, Hetzer's turf and home of The Jim Hetzer Theatrical Agency, we were in a parade, riding through Huntington's streets in costume, on convertibles–reminiscent of when the circus came to town. And come they did; the fairgrounds were always packed. But, in spite of the crowds, we always had a few passes for friends or relatives. One of the elevator operators at my hotel asked if I had any "Annie Oakleys." I said I'd try to get him one. But first I had to find out what it was. His face lit up when I gave him a pass to get into our show.

One Sunday afternoon in Sedalia, Missouri, I went to dinner with two of the singers. It was a day off and we went to a very nice restaurant, the lighting of which was on the dark side. I was dressed up and in high heels; and since it was so dark, I had my first cocktail in Sedalia, MO–a frozen daiquiri. It went down like lemonade.

Next on our travel agenda was Charleston, West Virginia, and then onto Indianapolis, Indiana, where I celebrated my 17th birthday; then to our final destination, Nashville, Tennessee, home of the seventh President of the United States, Andrew Jackson. Nashville wasn't as big a center as it is now for Country-Western music, but we did visit Jackson's home, The Hermitage, and The Parthenon, an exact replica of the one in Greece.

During out twelve-week gig I managed to save a little money, splurging only on a grey wool skirt that I bought in Iowa, some great purple sunglasses bought in Indianapolis, and my F.W. Woolworth cowgirl hat from Calgary.

Taking the train back home to Boston was both exciting and sad at the same time. I was anxious to tell my parents and friends all about my tour (although I had kept them posted with letters, postcards and phone calls throughout the tour), but I dreaded another school year.

But a promise is a promise. One of the requirements my mother insisted upon before agreeing to let me "go out west on a road show" was "You must come back and finish high school." I did, but my heart wasn't in it. Especially since now I had a love interest. Do dance, romance and algebra mix? Well, for me it was a difficult combination.

New York would have to wait while I was sitting out the next nine months at a desk in various classrooms at Lynn English High School in Lynn, Massachusetts.

Chapter 2

LYNN, LYNN, THE CITY OF SIN ONCE YOU GO OUT, YOU CAN'T GET IN

At 10:55 p.m. on August 31, 1941, I came into the world–just in time for the 11 o'clock news. The news of the day might have made most babies want to go back into the womb. It was the start of World War II, and two days before my birth Hitler and Mussolini concluded a five-day meeting that dealt with war plans. The Federal Government had lifted its restrictions on gasoline delivery, enabling motorists to fill their gas tanks for the Labor Day weekend. When the pains began, mom thought Labor Day came early that year. On Broadway, Gertrude Lawrence was starring in "Lady in the Dark" and Gene Kelly was strutting his stuff in "Pal Joey."

One Sunday morning in early December, my dad went to the corner store for the Sunday paper. My mother said she almost dropped me while she was giving me a bath in the bassinet, when the news of the Pearl Harbor attack flashed over the radio.

Too young to be aware of the turmoil that was going on in the world, I do remember being very frightened for my mother when she lost a baby when I was about three years old. I stayed with an upstairs neighbor, who gave me graham crackers and milk, but they gave little comfort. I missed and was very worried about my mother. Daddy had taken her to the hospital, and I wondered when they would come back home.

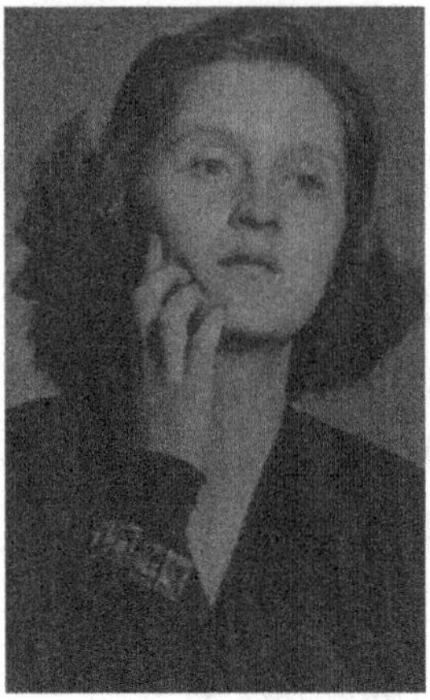

My Mother
Eleanor Beth Stevens Murphy

Mommy, Daddy, and me
Trying to do a passe' already

My Father
William Joseph Murphy

Mom and me at one of my first dance recitals. I remember the costume to this day. It was tangerine and gold satin with light blue ostrich feathers in my hat. I felt very glamorous.

Mom painted my brown Buster Brown oxfords gold with gold sprinkles on top. Taps were put on the soles.

Dad and me
After years of ballet class those turned in feet would turn out.

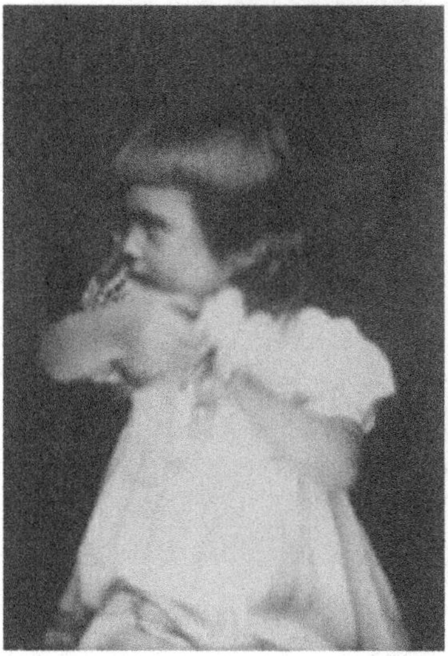

Ann holding black doll, Susie
circa 1943

Mom got me this black doll right before we went to South Carolina to visit my dad, who was stationed at Camp Croft. My doll's name was Susie and she wore a red and white checkered dress, red bows in her pigtails, white socks, and black Mary Jane shoes, and I loved her. All of my dolls were named Susie. I thought that was the most wonderful name a girl could have. I don't know if I heard Eddie Cantor singing "If You Knew Susie Likel I Know Susie" or what.

Me -circa 1943

Billy and me
At Revere Beach
circa-1953

From the author's personal collection

My best friend at Camp Wabunaki, Red (Ruth) Redland. Red and her brother, Woody, took me to my first baseball game at Fenway Park- a double header and the first game lasted thirteen innings. I must have liked it because the next day was Ladies' Day and we went back to the ballpark. Red is pictured in front of "Berry's Bump"- a 900 ft. hill, which traditionally Mt. Washington climbers would climb after the Mt. Washington climb. (6,288ft.) Camp Wabunaki was near Bridgton, Maine. I wish every kid in the world could go to a camp like this one.

My audition picture for the road show
THE INTERNATIONAL SPECTACULAR OF 1958
From the author's personal collection

My brother, Billy, on Amtrak back to Boston after seeing the show at RCMH.
photo by Tom St. John

The Waiter Number
photo by Tom St. John

The Calgary Stampede 1958
I was sixteen --- a young sixteen
from the author's personal collection

It is often a mysterious deciphering process to distinguish what one actually remembers from their early childhood years from what one was told about them while growing up. One famous, or infamous, incident was when I took my nude walk. Mom had put me in the backyard and had tied the rope of the clothesline onto the strap of my swimsuit. This enabled me to go twenty or thirty feet in each direction. But I escaped! I simply took off my sunsuit and paraded down Broad Street, a major street that runs right through Lynn. I was wearing nothing but shoes and socks, pushing an empty doll carriage, and on my way to see Aunt Nell. My mother always said to me, "You streaked before it was fashionable."

I streaked past Lucia's Grocery Store, and mom was furious that no one stopped me; they were all laughing uproariously. Panic-stricken she asked, "Have you seen Ann?" "She went that way," they laughed. Imagine her horror when she saw an empty sunsuit with no Ann in it, lying on the grass, attached to the clothesline. When she finally caught up with me, mom picked me up and somehow tried to cover me with the doll carriage.

As a little girl I had lots of dolls–named Susie, a name I thought was the most wonderful name a girl could have. I don't know if I'd heard Eddie Cantor singing "If You Knew Susie Like I Know Susie" or what, but to me Susie was a grand, fine name. I also had a teddy bear named Jerry that I'd named after a German Shepherd I'd met on the street one day.

We went to live with Aunt Nell (Helen), her husband Joe Tucker and Aunt Nell's brother Elmer Foster, when Daddy went overseas. This was Mom's side of the family, the Quakers. We lived on 48 Friend Street, right near the charming little Quaker Meeting House. Quaker Meeting was the antithesis of the highly theatrical Catholic church, where my dad's family went to Mass. So, I was raised in both churches–M&M–Mass and Meeting. One of my fondest memories of Quaker Meeting was the Saturday night church suppers of beans and franks. Beans and franks were a traditional Saturday night dish in the Boston area for years and years. That along with a glass of moxie, a very bitter tasting tonic, or soda or pop, depending on from which part of the country you came.

Aunt Nell would help with preparing the meal and washing the dishes. There must have been three hundred dishes or more. Uncle Elmer, who was quite the theatre devotee, used to talk about going to New York and I remember him saying "Radio City, Radio City" with such excitement. In my little girl mind, I envisioned a whole bunch of radios with little quarter notes and eighth notes jumping out of them.

Dad went into the Army and was stationed at Camp Croft in Spartanburg, South Carolina. My mother and I went down to visit him, and prior to one trip she very wisely got me a black doll. Naturally, her name was Susie. She had a red and white checkered dress, white socks, black Mary Jane shoes, and tiny red bows in her pigtails. I was just crazy about her.

We took the B&M (Boston & Maine) into Boston and went to South Station, where we got the train for New York. Leaving Penn Station, I thought New York was the most wonderful place in the world because I saw a Life Savers sign with the biggest Life Saver candies I'd ever seen; and, of course, I thought they were real. Wow!

Getting back to the tricks of childhood memories or hand-me-down stories that can play on the mind, Mom told me that I danced for all the porters in the dining car of the train. I think I remember that, vaguely. Once we got down there, Dad, Mom and I went to an outdoor concert where Dick Haymes and Margaret Whiting were singing. If I'm not mistaken, I think I danced there, too.

After basic training, Dad went to Italy on a troop ship and Mom and I settled in with Aunt Nell, Uncle Joe and Uncle Elmer. Now I wouldn't have to streak from 110 Green Street to see Aunt Nell; I'd be right there. I missed my father terribly. Often I'd go with my mom to her studio. She was an elocution teacher. I used to say she was an electric cushion teacher, and I'd ask her "Mom, do you have any pimples today?" I had not yet learned to say pupils.

I suppose the theatrical DNA is in me because my mother also had a radio program on WESX in Salem. She was the Saugus Community Hostess and my father used to write her scripts. Mommy and I would walk from Friend Street to Central Square to her studio and go upstairs. On the second floor, Mom's studio was right next to George's–the voice teacher. I was scared stiff of him; I'd hear him being very vocal and loud with his students. I shivered, "I'm glad I'm not in there with him." And it took me a long, long time–years even, for me to get over my fear of singing in public.

But there was one place I did want to be. Diagonally across from my mother's studio was her girlfriend's studio, Phyllis Galloway, the very pretty dance teacher. It was love at first curtsy. Little girls love big girls, and I certainly loved my first dance teacher and dancing.

A lady named Helen played the piano for the dance classes. One day, I was about four at the time, I went over to the piano and said "Oh, Helen, I just love your gold earrings. They match your teeth so beautifully." A couple of decades later I happened to be home on my week off from Radio City Music Hall and I spotted Helen at a bus stop. I approached her and spoke. Amazed that I remembered her, Helen asked "Oh Ann, how on earth did you ever recognize me?" I said "Oh, I recognized your gold earrings." She laughed saying "You mean they match my teeth?"

One of my first dance routines was a samba to "Tico Tico," the steps of which I remember to this day, and used many years later in the Palm Springs Follies, a musical review that dealt and played to the World War II era. And I thought the epitome of when one had arrived was when one could do toe tap, which is actually a very ugly form of dance. It mixes metaphors combining tap steps while one is on pointe.

One of my first recitals I remember, my costume was tangerine colored satin with a gold trim, and a few light blue ostrich feathers in my little hat. I had brown (probably Buster Brown) oxford shoes that my mother had spray-painted gold, with gold sprinkles (stardust) on them and taps on the souls. I felt so very glamorous.

Then there were our trips into Boston, where Mom and I would go to the movies. One day we went to see "Gilda" starring Rita Hayworth and Glen Ford. For weeks I ran around in my underpants, putting my long brown hair up and singing "Put The Blame On Mame, Boys." I should have practiced harder, because on November 9, 1965, I made my New York City singing debut at Radio City Music Hall during the blackout that crippled the northeast part of the country singing "Put The Blame On Mame, Boys." (But more about that later.)

On one trip into Boston, I was fascinated by the pictures of strippers outside The Old Howard Theatre in Scully Square. Mom yanked me away, but thanks to Uncle Joe, who worked at the Olympia Theatre in downtown Lynn, I must have seen the movie Pinocchio dozens of times. I just loved Pinocchio and believe I was highly influenced by the song "Hi-Diddle-Dee-Dee" (an actor's life for me).

President Truman gave the orders for the bombing of Hiroshima on August 6, 1945, and Nagasaki on August 9, 1945. Daddy was overseas.

When Dad was discharged from the Army, Mom and I went into Boston to meet him. We were dashing from South Station to North Station to catch the train to Lynn. With each parent holding one of my hands, I was running between them and struggling to keep up with them. "C'mon Ann, hurry up," they'd say. It wasn't until they saw a little boy pointing at me and laughing that they looked down and realized that my underpants had fallen down to my ankles.

Sometimes the Saturday night dinners would be at Aunt Nell's. She would soak the beans the night before on an oil burner and bake them in the oven, a hot black belly stove (wonderful in the winter when we'd play outside in the snow and our socks and mittens were soaked; we'd put our feet up toward the oven to warm up). And the turkey soup Aunt Nell made was the best I've ever had. I always vowed that when I got on my own and had my own place, I was going to try to make Aunt Nell's turkey soup. And one day I did! Mom cautioned me to strain the fat off; otherwise, I'd have diarrhea for a week. I had the most select pieces of turkey stewing, the carrots, onions and celery were simmering along, and in less than a second I blew it. I added a whole box of Minute Rice. The rice ate the turkey, the celery, the onions and the carrots. I didn't know that the rice was going to multiply and have babies. I had enough rice to feed the entire population of mainland China. Sitting there on the kitchen stool, I cried and cried.

On Sunday afternoons, Dad, Mom and I would go out to dinner. I'd wear a white Sunday dress, a pinafore, and I insisted upon wearing my dad's water canteen from the army---très chic.

After months at Aunt Nell's, who by the way, used to put me on her lap and dazzle me with stories of Cinderella, and stories of when she was a young girl "down East" (referring to Maine); finally we moved to our own place, a three-decker tenement on Story Avenue.

Another movie outing I remember was seeing "Three Little Girls in Blue" in which the song "On the Boardwalk in Atlantic City" was sung. The film starred June Haver, Vivien Blaine, Vera Ellen (a Rockette at one time), Celeste Holm, George Montgomery, Frank Latimore and Charles Smith. There was a scene in the movie that took place on a farm with lots of chickens. About a week later I came down with the chicken-pox and I was certain I'd gotten chicken-pox from the chickens in the "Three Little Girls in Blue."

A typical childhood, we played cowboys and cowgirls in "the old field," dreaming of becoming Roy Rogers and Dale Evans when we grew up. Climbing the apple tree behind Story Avenue was also a favorite hangout.

One day I was out in the backyard playing with Bobby Madigan when my very pregnant mother asked me to come inside as I had been instructed, when the time came to do so. The time had come; her water had broken and she had called my dad to come home from work. The three of us got into a taxi and the first stop was Lynn Hospital, where Mom and Dad got out and I went on to stay with Aunt Fanny in Peabody. Aunt Fanny was my paternal grandmother's sister and she was married to Warren Andersen. Later that afternoon, Aunt Fanny told me my mother had a baby boy. I had a brother.

I think I was in Peabody for a week, but it felt like an eternity, especially one Friday afternoon when a priest was visiting Aunt Fanny. She had served me lunch and I was sitting there between the two adults when the priest cautioned my aunt, "You'd better watch her; she's drinking all her chocolate milk and not eating her salmon." "Oh, excuse me, Father," she said, and off she went with my chocolate milk. So, there I was not feeling very kindly towards the priest, looking and making grimace faces at that salmon and, quite frankly, I haven't been particularly fond of salmon since.

That evening Uncle Warren came home from work and Aunt Fanny served supper, which included a salad, which included cucumbers, which Uncle Warren disliked. I never could figure out why he grew them if he didn't like them. Uncle Warren had a huge garden, which housed a watermelon patch and a grapevine, not to mention lots of vegetables. "Oh, I'll take the cucumbers right out, dear," Aunt Fanny said. There was no justice for a six year old. If he didn't have to eat his cucumbers, why did I have to eat my salmon?

It was pre-arranged that I would stay in Peabody about a week, but that Sunday my dad came to pick me up just for the day, to meet my new baby brother and see my mom. Dad told me on the bus ride to Lynn how much I was going to like Billy. I was nervous and excited, and when I walked into the Story Avenue living room my mother was lying resting on a couch with a multi-colored afghan she had crocheted during her pregnancy over her; and across the room on an opposite couch, lying in a bassinet, was my new baby brother sleeping peacefully. Dad said, "You can touch him if you want to."

I touched his little finger and, with all the pathos I could muster, turned to my parents and asked, "Do I have to go back to Peabody?" They had a comforting kind of laugh when they said "No."

The next six years were growing up years with all the typical trials, tribulations and fun times of children. Because we lived on a fairly busy street, traffic wise, my father would not allow me to have a bicycle, and I wanted one so badly.

Every Tuesday was stamp day in school, and for 10 cents each we could purchase a United States Savings Stamp and try to fill a book that would add up to $18.75; that plus a nickel would buy a United States Savings Bond. That practice of buying savings stamps stayed with me in later years when I worked at Radio City Music Hall. I'd go to the Rockefeller Center Post Office with any loose change I had in my pocket and buy some U.S. Savings Stamps and fill a book. How I wish the Federal Government would bring back those stamps.

I had accumulated about $6.10 and said to my father, "Well, Dad, if you won't let me have a bike, I'm going to get a puppy." So I cashed in my stamps and my mom went to the pet store and came back with Tippy. A black mongrel with a little white on her neck and paws, she was a love. And when she was a young lady, she was in love, or in lust, or in heat, because one fine night she had five puppies in bed with me. We told my dad that Tippy had had her period, but he didn't believe us.

On that particular night, Billy was in bed with my mother and I was sleeping in Billy's bed. I was on my side and felt a little stirring beside me, which I naturally thought was Tippy; but when I went to pat her, my hand went down across this body that was too short and went onto the sheet. I reached up and put on the overhead light, and there was one little squealing puppy beside me that I had just patted and another one at the foot of the bed. There was blood all over the bed. Tippy was panting, so I yelled out to my father, "Daddy, Daddy, Tippy had her puppies!" He came running into the room in his shorts and in typical male vocalize said, "Oh, Jesus Christ, she did. Wake up your mother."

Billy had slept through the whole thing while my mother and I made up a bed for Tippy and the pups. The next morning was a school day, and when Billy woke up he wanted to pick up one of the puppies, but my parents were afraid that Tippy, protecting her puppies, might bite Billy. It was just as though that dog understood what they were saying. To our amazement, she picked up one of the pups and brought it to my brother's feet.

There were other animals that made an appearance in the Murphy household. One Easter we had a rabbit and six chickens. And there was a time when Aunt Nell's brother, Uncle Elmer took me to the circus and bought me a lizard. So I came home from Ringling Brothers with a chameleon. We named him Felix. One night during suppertime there was a knock at the door. Dad had hamburger on his fork, just ready to enter his mouth, when the neighborhood kids came into the kitchen. One of them was holding a dead fly between his thumb and index finger exclaiming, "Mr. Murphy, Mrs. Murphy, we have a fly for Felix." Dad said to Mom, "Oh Steve, that thing has to go." (My mother's maiden name was Stevens; Dad always called her Steve.) So, Felix had to go. Oh, how I cried and carried on.

Mommy and I took Felix over to the old field to release him, my mother assuring me that he was going to work his way to Florida by following the railroad tracks and become a big alligator. Of course, she pointed north, toward Rockport, but what did I know? A few weeks later another traumatic event occurred. Some men were in the old field with big derricks plowing the field. I ran over frantically to tell them to be careful where they dug because my baby alligator was working his way to Florida. The told me they would be very careful.

Thus, life was pretty routine until my eighth grade. My parents had been arguing constantly. It was extremely difficult and intense; I never knew when I sat down to dinner whether or not a fight would erupt. One early morning my mother took Billy and me to Cousin Mary's (Aunt Nell's niece) florist shop. We used to go there often and ride with Cousin Mary when she would make floral deliveries, or sometimes we'd be in the back of the store and make corsages out of scraps of fern and flowers.

I did not think too much of it that particular day. Although I did, at one point, think we were there for an exceptionally long time. When my mother came in to get us that afternoon around 5:00 p.m., I remember Cousin Mary saying to her, "Well, I hope you know what you're doing, Eleanor."

We walked out of the florist shop, up Broad Street and into a different apartment. There was all of our furniture, and Mommy said, "We're not going to live with Daddy anymore." Though I had been shocked and saddened (the wind had been knocked out of my sails), I knew deep down inside that it was inevitable. This was in late June and two days later I was shipped off to camp.

Camp Wabunaki was about eight miles northwest of Bridgton, Maine. It was a private girls' camp and I spent four of the most wonderful summers of my life there. To this very day I look back upon it with wonderful, cherished memories. I wish every kid in the world could go to a camp like I did. And that is quite a testimony to Camp Wabunaki, which was superbly run by Charles and Mildred Leader (affectionately known as Uncle Chuck and Aunt Chick) of Sugar Hill, New Hampshire, as I went to camp under very adverse circumstances.

In fact, many years later, after I had been in the Rockettes a few years, my mother and I went for a visit to Wabunaki. My best friend from camp, Ruth Redland (Red) was then a counselor there. How I loved that place and seeing Aunt Chick and Red. (Uncle Chuck had died a few years earlier.) In spite of my show biz career, I have always loved the country more than the city. When it came time for us to leave the camp and me go back to work in New York City, I didn't want to leave. That prompted my mother to say, "What do you want to do, dance in the woods?"

Red and I reminisced about our campfire memories, skinny dipping in Lake Hancock, climbing Mt. Chocorua, Mt. Cannon, Mt. Adams and the pièce de résistance, Mt. Washington, the highest mountain east of the Mississippi river and north of the Carolinas. But by far, the most difficult climb was "Adams Slide," a trail ascending Mt. Adams. The river trips were more relaxing, canoeing up the Saco River or down the Crooked River, and camping out on their sandy little river beaches.

The night before each trip Uncle Chuck would tell us a story relating to where we were going, which usually dealt with the land once belonging to the Indians. One time Mommy and Billy paid a visit to Wabunaki. The camp was on a man-made peninsula enveloped with balsam, pine and white birch trees. Billy, just five or six years old at the time, insisted there were Indians on the land. He happened to wander over to the counselors' shack where they stored the archery bows and arrows, and came running out exclaiming, "I found them! I found them!"

At camp we often managed to get into a little trouble. One night after taps, we snuck down to the waterfront where we had chapel service every morning and learned of the planned activities for the day-be it swimming, sailing, canoeing, tennis, archery, arts & crafts or horseback riding. We meant no patriotic disrespect, but in a gale of giggles we raised our bras up the flagpole. The next morning when everyone went to Pledge Allegiance to the Flag, two embarrassed campers (not us) had to take down the bras before raising the flag. We were also in love with Jackie, one of the two very handsome sons of Aunt Chick and Uncle Chuck, and we'd volunteer to roll the tennis courts just so we could pick up his cigarette butts.

Sunday, after an early dinner, was musical appreciation day. Girls would play piano-Chopin, Mozart, Bach, Beethoven or Tchaikovsky,and I would dance. But the same girls performed all the time. I decided I would get my whole cabin involved, so I wrote a skit in which I played a sailor who was told to mop the deck. While mopping, I told my ship mates about wanting to get a tattoo and sang "A Sailor's Not A Sailor 'Til a Sailor's Been Tattooed" from Irving Berlin's "There's No Business Like Show Business." That segued into "A Whale of a Tale" from "20,000 Leagues Under the Sea." To me, music was music, and if you appreciated it, it didn't matter if it was Bach or Berlin. To my embarrassment, the next day Jackie Leader, the man with whom I was passionately in love said, "A Sailor's Not A Sailor 'Til a Sailor's Been Tattooed"-what a thing to sing for Sunday Musical Appreciation!" I was mortified. I think I also offended a couple of religions, too. I was banned—banned in Bridgeton.

My friend Red came from Newton, Massachusetts and was an army brat, the daughter of Colonel Arthur J. Redland and his wife, Ruth. Her mom and dad were so nice to me when I visited their beautiful home, and Red and her brother Woody took me to my very first baseball game at Fenway Park. It was a double-header (Red Sox vs. Kansas City Athletics) and the first game lasted 13 innings. I must have liked it because the next day was Ladies Day and we went back to Fenway again. We sat next to the ballplayers' bull pen. Great baseball players–Jackie Jensen, Jimmy Pearsall, Sammy White and, of course, number 9, Ted Williams. We two boy-crazy girls came out of the park with a sunburn down one side of our faces.

High school was both scary and fun. Scary to me because I was so painfully shy, in spite of the fact that I played Cinderella in the school play in my Junior year. Perhaps it was a reaction to all the domestic problems, but I became very withdrawn and tongue-tied. Someone would say to me, "Say something," which would make matters worse because I had nothing to say, unless I was giving an oral composition for English or Speech class, or performing on stage. In my Senior year, I entered the Declamation Contest, and a young man I liked, Richard Darsney Cook, did a cutting from the Archibald MacLeish play "JB" and won, deservedly so. He was nothing short of excellent. Our beloved speech teacher, Mary Ishkanian, coached all of us through this oratorical process.

I had a part-time job and was paying for some of my dance classes, taking about ten classes a week. Geraldine Paré and Dot and Bob Cannessa were my teachers; Geraldine gave me private lessons and ballet class with Dot, and jazz and tap with Bob. Dot and Bob's studio at the time was right across from Fisherman's Beach in Swampscott. It was wonderful to take a ballet barre class while looking at the ocean.

At school my math and science background was not good at all, but English and speech were a different story. The quiet mouse loved them both, especially when it came time to deliver a prepared speech. But after painful math classes and sliding by in other classes, graduation day finally came into the horizon. My date for the Senior Prom,

Jackie Gilbo, kept telling me "we're going to stay out 'till 3 o'clock in the morning." That was definitely 'the thing to do' because post-prom, the next day, the question on everyone's lips was "and what time did you get in?" The later the hour, the more looked-on-with-awe the person was. However, since I had been out on that road show, and had been exposed to the show business night-life and parties, staying out to the wee hours of the morning meant nothing to me. It still doesn't. After the 11 o'clock news, I'm ready for bed.

The day after graduation, I headed back to New York City. Working as an usherette at the Stanley Warner Theatre (becoming very familiar with the score of "Porgy and Bess"), it would be a long, hot summer of pounding the pavements; and just after my eighteenth birthday, I prepared to join the "Israeli Army"

Chapter 3

TWENTY MINUTES TO OVERTURE; STAND BY, PLEASE, TWENTY MINUTES TO OVERTURE, STAND BY

The small rehearsal hall was located on the seventh floor of Radio City Music Hall, diagonally across from the large rehearsal hall that had floor marking mimicking the Great Stage; and had just enough room for the line of thirty-six to fit across the room from stage-left to stage-right. The entire symphony orchestra was squeezed into that small rehearsal hall. From the tinniest flute, to the trumpeting tuba, to the tempo-beating timpani, the musicians were tightly packed. We were rehearsing the Israeli show entitled "Happy Land," which would open on September 24th, 1959.

Totally awestruck and scared out of my wits, I witnessed one of the most exciting scenarios of my young life. Senior producer Leon Leonidoff, in his thick Russian accent said to lead orchestra conductor Raymond Paige, director of the Radio City Music Hall Symphony Orchestra, "Rrraymond, Rrraymond, the overture .iit lacks something, iit lacks a piddle." Raising his baton in the air and not missing a beat, Paige responded with, "Well, Leon, 'piddle' is not a musical term." Paige also used to get a kick out of telling the musicians to "Go to L!" The orchestral score would be marked off with alphabet letters every several measure or so. From that Wednesday on, I always went to orchestra rehearsal. In fact, I would sit right under the high hat snare drums (Irv Levine on drums); and after the Rockettes taught me how to knit, I'd be sitting there knitting beneath the crashing cymbals. The musicians called me Madame Defarge.

When I say I was scared stiff; I was! That tension was lifted a bit when Rockette Jean Mullenix of Matoon, Illinois said to me at an early Monday morning on-stage rehearsal, "Ann, you're only hurting yourself. Relax. God, when I first came here I was scared shit-stiff." I was always grateful to Jeannie for the calming words and the laugh. (Early morning rehearsals were scheduled between 7:00 a.m. and 10:00 a.m. because that was the only time the stage was available, before the first movie screening of the day began.)

Many months and early morning rehearsals later, Emily corrected me stating, "Ann, you always look as though you're ahead of the line. Step back a little." (In lineup, we always had to toe the dotted line.) When I told Jeannie, "I don't understand it; I am toeing the line." Jean came up with a good one again. She said, "You are toeing the line, Ann. Your bust are heeling it!"

Rockette rehearsal pianist Beula Crangle pounded the ivories of the Steinway as Russell Markert's assistant Emilia Sherman put the "Israeli Army" regiment through their steps. The new shows always opened on a Thursday, and the opening day was determined by the size of the house a few weeks prior to the openings.

At my first Monday morning prep rehearsal prior to the Thursday opening, we were making little spokes of a wheel, where each girl came from an open formation position to her respective place in the spoke of the wheel. Well, this little "Israeli soldier" went into the wrong spoke, between two girls where I was not supposed to be. Dance captain Duffey stood up for me and explained to Emily, "She got mixed up; they all looked alike to her."

Since we were in rehearsal clothes–various colored leotards and tights–Emily shot back, "Well, on opening day they're all really going to look alike; they'll be in costume, dressed alike." Occasionally things would go wrong and things and people would get mixed up crazily on stage. Dancers would somehow end up in the wrong places, or bars of music might be missing. Coming off stage, into the wings one day when things had gone askew, Ann Kalman said, "Gee, that was fun; I saw people out there I hadn't see in years."

Emily had explained to us the reason the Music Hall uses the terms "prompt" and "OP" (opposite of prompt). She said that there were so many people involved on stage that when she gave an order to move a little to the right or left, she didn't want some little Suzie Q asking, "Your right or my right?" I wanted to ask what's to prevent us from asking "your prompt or my prompt," but I decided to refrain from asking the question and just shivered in my tap shoes.

My opening day on the Great Stage came about on September 24, 1959 in "The Happy Land," The Israeli Show, and was I ever one nervous little soldier. So nervous, in fact, that I got out of step but the girl behind me, Jane Freund, sounded out the counts and I quickly got back into step. What nerves can do. People often ask, "Do you ever make a mistake?" Well, Rockettes are human, after all. It happens but not often and, hopefully, not noticeably. It's far better to miss a kick than to kick out, which is when one girl kicks and the other thirty-five do not. Whenever a girl would miss a kick, much harder to see, Emily would catch everything and after the show she would go to the girl who missed the kick and say, "You owe me a kick."

As lady soldiers of the Israeli army, the Rockettes wore white short sleeve blouses with a band across our shirts to carry our rifles, short white pleated skirts, white bobby socks over our beige opera hose tights, gold tap shoes and a red beret. In song, we were introduced by the stunning and sexy Israeli singer Shoshana Damari, who sang "Kalaniot" (red poppies), to which we also danced. "Kalaniot" was written for Miss Damari by Moshe Wilensky in 1944. A graduate of Warsaw State Conservatory, he had settled in Palestine in 1932. Miss Damari was born in the town of Damar in Yemen, from which her rabbi father, her mother and four siblings had to flee to Israel. With a rough childhood behind her, she dazzled Radio City Music Hall audiences and me.

Preceding the ballet number, two bearded Yemenites, did a crazy body wiggling Middle Eastern dance. One of these young dancers was named Nehemia Sharabi. It all started when another Rockette and I were seated with Nehemia and his dance partner down in the Music Hall cafeteria. I was teaching them English, when one of them exclaimed "Jesus Christ." "Oh, don't learn that English," I said. Rockette Sue Bono laughed herself silly.

Nehemia proposed marriage, but maybe he thought I had proposed to him. It was a mistake in the language barrier. We were talking over the phone one day and I said to him in a typically American way, "Why don't you give me a ring the first of the week?" There was a long pause–a silence. Finally, he asked, "Vhat do you vant me to give you?" "Oh no," I cried, "in America we have this expression . . ." Well, a week later he proposed. No wonder there are international mix-ups.

Another beautiful song sung by Miss Damari was "Orcha Bamidbar" (A Camel Caravan in the Desert). One can just visualize a lonely camel caravan crossing the desert, while listening to this music. How terribly sad, and what a tragedy that there is still so much turmoil in this troubled part of the world, where it is so rich in its music with its enharmonic minor scale, its art and its rich history. The Israeli show ran for four weeks, so it was only one week into to the show (I was just getting the hang of it) when we started rehearsals for the next new show.

My second Rockettes show showcased the film "A Summer Place" starring Troy Donahue, Sandra Dee,

Dorothy McGuire and Richard Egan. It was a love story where a troubled, unmarried teen becomes pregnant. In the final scene, Dee and Donahue are married and they kiss on the dock where Dee utters the famous line "in front of God and everyone?" We were glamorous scarecrows in this one.

Besides the Music Hall traditions of the annual Christmas show with its Nativity Pageant and at Easter, the Glory of Easter Pageant, there were also backstage traditions. After an exhausting opening day usually beginning with a 7:00 a.m. dress rehearsal, and ending at 10:30 p.m., the exhausted Rockettes would break into song. Their traditional opening-day dressing room song, sung to the tune of "Good Mornin' Good Mornin'" from "Singing in the Rain" was:

> Good night, good night
> We've danced the whole day through.
> Good night, good night, to you and you and you.
> Good night, good night
> I'm pooped and so are you
> Good night, good night to you.
> When we leave the Music Hall
> Our feet are mighty sore.
> But it's better to do our kicks each day
> Than be a low-down whore.
> Good night, good night
> I'm pooped and so are you
> Good night, good night to you - and you - and YOU!

Another fun little backstage gig was when older Rockettes would tell a new girl that they couldn't find the key to the Contour Curtain, and they couldn't start the show without it. A frantic fledgling Rockette would run all over the theatre looking for the lost contour key. Reminiscent of a snipe hunt, eh?

Regarding Radio City Music Hall statistics on the Great Stage, there are four stage elevators, including the orchestra pit. These stage elevators are known as hydraulic lifts; each lift is 70 feet wide and 16 feet deep. Each lift can go down as low as 28.75 feet below stage level and 14 feet above stage level. Within three of the stage elevators is a turntable, which is 43 feet in diameter and can go up or down, fast or slow, right or left. Behind the 100 foot arched proscenium opening the stage width is about 140 feet wide and 64 feet deep.

The "key" to presenting this "sunburst" opening is the rising of the 3,000 pound gold-colored 60 foot high and 110 foot wide contour curtain, which is raised and lowered by thirteen 7.5 horsepower, reversible, 220-volt, 3 phase electric motors. The contour curtain is virtually a performer in itself, perhaps an acrobat. For example, the curtain can be raised at one point and lowered at another simultaneously, or arched over a single entertainer, or be made to go up diagonally in step with music. The performance is accomplished by observing 13 moving "position indicators" and by proper manipulation of 42 batteries, 26 sliding limit switches, and a "master-single" throw switch.

There is also a steam curtain and a rain curtain. In order to use the steam curtain, one has to "bleed" the steam–let it ooze a little. For the rain curtain, a ground cloth must be placed on number one elevator, and we have a rain affect in true Gene Kelly "I'm Singin' In The Rain" fashion. In order to accomplish this, the number one elevator is lowered imperceptibly. After the curtain comes down, giant fans are placed on the elevator to dry off the water before the next show. The auditorium used to seat 6,200 people; it is now down to 5800 seats.

Before we knew it, the Christmas Season was upon us and the Christmas Show opened with a Cary Grant film, "Operation Petticoat." We Rockettes were spacemen, or space-girls, if you will, and were costumed in gold lamé one-piece sleeveless leotard-like suits with flowing capes. On our heads we wore football helmets that were spray-painted gold, and on top of each helmet were three antennae. At one weekday matinee my antennae got caught on another dancer's antennae during the final pose for the bow. She had to exit in one direction, and I another. To disentangle myself, I went charging toward the prompt wing; there were 35 girls together, and me, several feet away from them. I quickly ducked into the wings, while two ladies in the audience's front row were laughing hysterically. And so the shows came and went. The days were long, but the years went by quickly.

The Christmas Show, as does Christmas in real life, always denoted the passing of another year. Besides the hustle and bustle of every day life, what with the shopping between shows, four and sometimes five shows a day, with the Christmas shows came the animals and adventure. The Music Hall animal room housed three camels, a horse or two, three donkeys and several sheep. These animals were used during the Nativity Pageant. Occasionally, interesting things would happen on our pilgrimage to Bethlehem.

Beginning on stage-right (excuse me–prompt), actors and animals would follow the Star of David across the "desert" to the birthplace of the Christ child. We were all dressed in biblical types of robes and would proceed across the stage; many of us would wait in the OP wings to make a re-entrance after the rising of the scrim to bow and kneel at the foot of Mary, Joseph and the Baby. Obstreperous camels sometimes had different ideas about the whole production.

One year on a Catholic holiday, the Feast of the Immaculate Conception, parochial school kids had off from school and the house was packed. A battalion of Roman soldiers, complete with bows and arrows, followed the bucking, prancing, kicking, spitting, jumping all over the place camel. The camel then stopped, faced upstage, with its head away from the audience and its hind legs spread-eagle toward the audience, and peed and pooped all over the stage. (They could have used the rain curtain at this juncture). Soldiers were marching time in place and, I don't know how they did it, but the entire symphony orchestra played the same bars of Adeste Fidelis (O Come All Ye Faithful) over and over again with the string section bowing their fiddles towards the audience and arching away from the spraying camel. Uproarious laughter came from the house and stage managers were climbing the curtains. If Governor Nelson Rockefeller had been there himself, there was nothing he could have done.

Two more camel incidents come to mind. In one, I was to follow a group of soldiers, leaving a few feet of space between the soldiers and myself. The Camel was supposed to follow me with a few safe feet between me and it. But sometimes the camel would be right behind me, and I would be running up closer to the soldiers, leaving no space between them and me. Consequently, I was getting corrections to please keep a distance from the soldiers. I wonder if the camel was getting corrections, too. This camel was a young male who had not been gelded yet, so when the girls had their periods, one had to be particularly careful.

In the beginning years there was an animal trainer named Frank. A small-framed guy, he was known to go out between shows and imbibe a few. (If I had to take the camel across the stage, I would have had a few, too.) Anyway, during one show we were standing in the wings in our biblical garb, and across the stage came Frank with this camel jumping like a gazelle, legs going out all over the place. Frank uttered under his whiskey breath, "You're going to get it, you little bastard." One year there was a very small camel causing Leonidoff to shriek from the house during a dress rehearsal morning, "Jesus Christ, the camel looks like a cockroach."

Then there's a story handed down over the ages. If it isn't true, it's sure a good one. The tale has it that they were doing a tableau of "The Last Supper." The stage was set with the twelve apostles all there. With a 100 foot proscenium, just twelve people on the Music Hall stage could look like molecules. Leon shouted, "Get more people on the stage." An embarrassing silence followed. Finally someone went up to Leon and said, "Leon, there were only twelve apostles there." "Oh vell, ve'll change it then," Leon shrieked. Leon also used to say. "I don't get ulcers; I give them." But with all his funny-isms, Leon was a brilliant stage producer and really knew how to dress the stage.

In December 1960 I got to be a toy soldier and marched with thirty-five other toy soldiers. We were doing the famous and classic Parade of the Wooden Soldiers, brilliantly choreographed by Russell Markert who, in this particular show was also the producer. The accompanying film was "The Sundowners" starring Deborah Kerr and Robert Mitchum. Because the film was a lengthy one, the stage show was shorter, but what an adorable and heartfelt show. "Holiday Wishes" was its name and, conceived by Russell, it really conveyed the kindness and gentle nature of his soul.

Santa Claus found Aladdin's magic lamp and was offered three wishes. His first wish was to go to "Candyland," where the Music Hall Corp de Ballet, choreographed by Margaret Sande, found the ballet girls dressed in tutus that looked like ribbon candy. Dazzling Helen Wood was the soloist who danced with a big bowl and spoon while doing pirouettes and licking the frosting before a grand jeté. His second wish was to fly. "Up in the Air" featured The Choraleers and The Kovacs, a trampoline act. His third wish was the introduction to the Rockette march "Under the Tree." The lovely words that Santa spoke were:

> "Peace on Earth; Good Will Towards Men
> Let's Make This World A Safe Place
> For Each Girl and Boy
> And, If Only, All The Soldiers in the World
> Were Made Of Toy."

Ta Da! The intro into The Parade of the Wooden Soldiers began.

I have never forgotten that introduction; I've always loved it. I don't know who wrote those lines, whether Russell or Albert Stillman, the Music Hall lyricist, but I asked Russell for permission to use it on my Christmas card that year, which he granted.

Over the years I had marched the Parade of the Wooden Soldiers hundreds of times when, one day I heard for the first time the beautiful, lilting counter-melody played by the string section as the two vertical lines of eighteen soldiers were marching to meet one another center-stage in preparation for moving into the six-spoke wheel. This famous climax of the routine was, of course, the fall, when all the soldiers fall down in a domino action after having a cannon go off issuing a loud blast. Being on the end and the last to fall, I landed on a big, bright red pillow, quickly put there by a worried Santa before the fall reached me. So I always had a soft landing (well, almost always).

Today's Rockettes are still marching to the Parade of the Wooden Soldiers and thrilling audiences as much as ever, continuing the holiday tradition of this wistful and heartfelt routine.

One Christmas season, there was no vacancy in the animal room. It was occupied by a pretty large young lady, a nine year old Asian elephant named Tanya. The other animals took over our quick-change room and even spilled out into the hallway. Not only did I have the pleasure of riding Tanya, I also rode up in the passenger elevator with her–your average Otis elevator. Though she was only nine years old, she was big enough to fill that elevator car all by herself. With another Rockette, Barbara Ann Cittadino and Tanya's trainer Jenda Smaha, Tanya and I ascended the floors so that Tanya could go up to the roof for a fresh air walk. Barbara entered the elevator first; then the elephant backed-in, pinning Barbara at Tanya's rear end and causing her to exclaim, "Oh, I'm gonna have a heart attack; I'm gonna have a heart attack!" Jenda and I were positioned alongside each of Tanya's front legs, me trying to be as skinny as possible, pulling in those boobs and asking Tanya what she wanted for Christmas.

Tanya was born in Thailand; she had beautiful eyelashes (hers real; mine were false) and a beautiful disposition. One day she hit the guide wire while going on stage. It frightened her quite a bit but, trouper that she was, she overcame it and was always on time for her entrance in the finale. Like the camel, Tanya had an accident on stage one day. Jenda and his beautiful wife Rena would really let Tanya know when they were displeased with her. When I stepped into the animals' room to visit Tanya, Jenda and Rena said, "We're not talking to her today. We're mad at her because of what she did on stage." I looked at Tanya and she shook her head "No" as if to say, "Don't listen to them."

Everyone loved Tanya; she was gentle and sweet. When she'd come out to the backstage area from the animal room, she would sit on the pin-rail near the water cooler, and sometimes she'd make her way to the stage managers' drawer where one of the crew would slip her some sugar. I gave her a bag of carrots for Christmas; the whole bag was gone in less than a minute. (Like M&M candies for us.)

Other personality animals included Reuben, the sheep who had an identity crisis. Reuben had been the little lamb in the Broadway production of "Gypsy," and the children in the show raised him as though he were a pet dog. Sheep are undemonstrative by nature, but Reuben would always greet an individual like a tail-wagging dog. Then there was the baby donkey named Daisy, who went around "goosing" everybody. You couldn't turn your back on Daisy. And we even celebrated a blessed event every once in a while in the backstage animal room. One morning, when the animal crew went to check on the animals, they found a little black baby lamb crouched in the hay in the camel bin. "He probably thought the camel was his daddy," said Rockette Carol Toman.

My parents often came down to New York for the shows, especially the Christmas shows. Billy often complained that "all we do is sit in the green room and go out and eat." An energetic young boy, waiting in the green room for the girls upstairs was not his thing–yet. In a few more years, that was a different story. One year Dad came down by himself, and while waiting for me to do the show, he went to Mass at St. Patrick's Cathedral. Sitting at the end of a pew, one of the church ushers tapped him on the shoulder, handed him the offering box and asked him to take up the collection. Pointing to a section near the rear of the church, he directed Dad saying, "You take up there; that's ole Jim Farley's group and the pickins should be good."

Come spring, came Easter with the traditional "Glory of Easter" pageant, produced by Leon Leonidoff and music by Anton Rubinstein, the "Kamenoi Ostrow." The "Glory of Easter" had a total ensemble cast accompanied by not only the Symphony Orchestra, but also the mighty Wurlitzer Organ. As the contour curtain rose on this majestic church-like setting, a lone candle lighter would walk across the altar and light the altar candles–first on stage-left, a genuflect in the center of the altar, then on stage-right, and exit. (Sometimes I played that role) The reason that I know the aforementioned stage statistics is that I married the control board operator, Tom St. John. If the applause came on the rising of the contour curtain, the applause belonged to Tom; but if it came on the genuflect, the applause was mine.

A solo soprano was statuesquely posed by the prompt organ consul and on stage the corp de ballet did very slow ballet movements all the while carrying Easter lilies. The ballet company was later joined by the Rockettes, who also carried Easter lilies, but were costumed differently, with the ballet wearing long blue, white and silver costumes, and the Rockettes in off-white and gold gowns with hats that were quite high and covered with off-white flowing chiffon. For some reason we called the Rockettes the "nuns," maybe because our hats somewhat resembled a nun's habit. We descended stairs coming down from the altar, which was on the raised second elevator, and joined the ballet. The climax of these balletic movements was the making of a human cross.

One year we had those wonderful little Austrian musicians, The Vienna Boys Choir. Upstage on the higher-raised third elevator, positioned on a series of three wide staircases, the Vienna Boys Choir sang their little hearts out. At stage-right and stage-left were several Rockette "nuns," lilies in hand, waiting for their musical cue to make their entrance by descending the stairs and joining the ballet on the remaining stage surface, which was on the number one elevator and the wood downstage of it.

I was the lead "nun" on stage-right and happened to glance upstage, when one of the little boys fainted. It was just a couple of moments before our entrance, but instinctively, I ran up to the boy, bent down and held him in my arms; I looked up at the rest of the singing boys and, in my one and only line in German, asked "Was ist los?" They all started speaking German to me! What did I expect? In the next instant, their leader came onstage and carried the tired, probably jet-lagged little boy offstage. They had just flown in the day before the opening. The little boy recovered and rejoined the choir for the next show.

I made my way back to my position to lead the Rockettes down the stairs, but in the process of playing Florence Nightengale the flowing chiffon of my "nun's habit" hat had fallen in front of my face. Then it was time for our descent, and as we descended the stairs, the hands behind me were reaching down and trying to pull the draping chiffon out of my face. But the more they pulled, the more it draped. To make matters worse, we had to side-step across the stage front-right just behind the footlights while the hands were still reaching for my veil. I looked like a defrocked nun, and the musicians in the string section were biting their lips to keep from laughing during this solemn religious pageant. Finally, the contour curtain came down, thank God and Tom.

In 1962 the Music Hall collaborated with Disney for the Easter show. Advance publicity had included several Allied Van Lines trucks with their sides painted "Moving Disneyland from Anaheim, California to New York's Radio City Music Hall" while traveling across the country with Mickey Mouse and cast and crew playing shopping centers as they made the 3,000 mile trek. They said people were asking, "Are they really moving Disneyland to Radio City Music Hall?"

An adorable show, both the "Glory of Easter" and the stage show titled "Disneyland USA" were produced by Leon Leonidoff. As customary, the show began with the Glory of Easter. After the contour curtain came down, the orchestra pit descended and, still playing, it came right back up again with Mickey Mouse conducting the orchestra. When organist Raymond Bohr asked Raymond Paige what music he wanted played on the organ between the feature film "Moon Pilot" and the stage show, Paige remarked, "Don't ask me; Mickey Mouse is conducting the overture!"

A funny thing happened on the way home from the theatre one night. It was May 19, 1962, a mild spring evening, and this particular night I had not taken off my stage makeup. I usually did so, but that night I must have been anxious to get out into the warm spring air. On the way home I was preparing to cross 45th Street and 8th Avenue (I lived at 325 West 45th St., the Whitby Apartments) when out of a clear blue sky something made me approach a policeman standing in the street directing traffic. I had noticed there was an exceptional amount of traffic and proceeded toward the policeman and said,

"Hi." He sighed an exasperated "Hi." As he was doing so, I happened to turn my head just enough to notice the marquee at Madison Square Garden, which at that time was at 8th Avenue and 50th Street.

"HAPPY BIRTHDAY JFK" it read. The policeman must have been a frustrated Republican or a very tired policemen, or both. "Well," I said kiddingly, "do you think I should go up there or should I go right home?"

To my amazement he replied, "Oh, go on up. Everybody's up there. Jack Benny's up there and everybody is up there. Everybody's having a ball up there."

So I quickly walked across the street, and went home to deposit my trench coat that I'd been carrying. I was wearing a black straight skirt and a variegated knit sweater that I had made, plus my stage makeup and maroon high heels; my hair was long and down. I trotted up to the Garden. The way the police officer had spoken, I thought it was the same sort of party that the late Mike Todd had thrown, where the whole world was invited. What a surprise I had when I walked to the front of the Garden and found myself facing approximately fifty policemen! "Well," I flirted, "I work for Governor Rockefeller and I think you should let me in." Before I knew it, I was doing cramp-roll time steps for them to help prove that I was a Rockette.

"OK kid, OK," they said. "Go around to the 49th St. stage door." I ran around to the stage door entrance and tried to make my way in but what I was up against there was even worse than fifty policemen. He was rather tall, slim and was damned if he was going to let me into the Garden. He started by saying, "I can't let you in; there are too many people in there already."

My only reply was, "But I'm thin; I don't take up too much room."

"Well," he said," it's not that. The fact is, you might be armed." So I held my arms up high so he could frisk me. He didn't. He missed his chance. The two of us stood there debating back and forth when, right before my eyes was placed a hundred dollar ticket to the party! I grabbed it, said thank you to the stage doorman who gave me the ticket and made the remark, "I'll vote for the man and not for the party," to which they replied, "That's right, honey, vote for the man and not for the party," and I made my way into the Madison Square Garden.

Just as I was entering, God rest her soul, Marilyn Monroe was exiting. A policeman was standing guard on the steps that led directly into the arena. I asked him if I could borrow a pen and proceeded to get Miss Monroe's autograph. Newspaper men were surrounding the woman, who looked like a jeweled goddess. She was just beautiful, dressed in a tight-fitting long, nudish-silver, diamond disked, beaded gown. In fact, the gentlemen of the press pushed me right into her. I was bosom-to-bosom with Marilyn Monroe! And all because of that policeman on 8th Avenue and 45th Street said, "Oh, go on up there."

If ever anyone could feel empathy towards another person, it was at this moment. I had never met this woman before in my life, but as she stood right before me I realized I was gazing at a very lonely, troubled person-beautiful, but tragic. One would think it would be a high to sing Happy Birthday to the President of the United States. But I could feel her sadness, and I was so awestruck at meeting this ravishing movie star that all I could mutter was, "Miss Monroe, may I have your autograph?" She had a motherly, protective quality about her as she seemed to pull me away from the press and toward her. She obliged, almost painfully, while quivering her lips in that uniquely Monroe style and saying to the press, "Don't push." I have always regretted that I didn't tell her how beautiful she looked and that I had always admired her—her acting and her wonderful style as a comedienne. She probably could have used the compliment.

Inside the Garden, President John F. Kennedy was giving his birthday "Thank you" to all who had given him a birthday salute. The party was arranged under the joint auspices of the Democratic National Committee, The Democratic State Committee, and the Citizens for Kennedy. It was the first time in my life I'd ever had a hundred dollar ticket to anything. I was so excited I don't think I sat in the seat for ten seconds.

As I was leaving the Garden a man approached me and asked if I had gotten the autographs. (I also got Shirley MacLaine's while inside.) He invited me to have a drink with him, which I did. We walked everywhere, but I did not get into a cab with him. He introduced himself as Larry Arnold and gave me his card, which said he was President of Global Relations Associates. He told me they got any commodity for any pro-western country. Larry invited me to Washington D.C. and I took the train down on my week off. He was very kind and took me to the Lincoln Memorial, the Smithsonian and to Arlington National Cemetery. I also got a taste for Washington night life, hitting The Shoreham and The Blue Mirror.

My dad always called me on Sundays and that Sunday morning in August 1962 I was speechless and so saddened when he told me that Marilyn Monroe was dead. Where were the compliments and love she needed so badly?

But nothing could have prepared us for November 22, 1963. We had just completed the first show of the day. Girls had gone out shopping or to lunch, and I was sitting at my dressing room place eating a peanut butter sandwich. With a shocked look on her face, Noreen Sheehan came running into the dressing room exclaiming, "Have you kids heard? Kennedy's been shot! People on the street are saying Kennedy's been shot." Immediately, I jumped up and turned on the television. There was Walter Cronkite, big as life, with a sober look on his face. It was approximately 12:40 p.m. Eastern Standard Time and we just knew that President Kennedy really had been shot. Twenty minutes later, with tears in his eyes, Mr. Cronkite announced that the President of the United States, John

Fitzgerald Kennedy was dead. We could not believe our ears. All the Rockettes were roaming around the dressing room sobbing hysterically. Emily Sherman found me in the hallway and we embraced each other while we cried unabashedly.

Those were the days when we did four shows a day with a film beginning the day, so there were five films a day and four stage shows. The audience out in the house was watching the second film of the day, unaware of the tragic history in the outside world.

When we went on stage to do the second show we were still crying. Barbara Di Matteo Douglas chastised the stage manager for not announcing to the house that the President had been killed. "How come you can announce when John Glen circled the world from outer space and you can't tell them the President has been shot?" "They'll find out soon enough, "said John Jackson, Director of Stage Operations.

We were wearing simple brown leotards and tights with white ruffled Cuban style sleeves. We were cigars, and when the curtain opened, we were discovered propped up in a high cigar box. Tears streamed down the faces of thirty-six Rockettes who went through the entire routine without even a hint of a smile. The audience must have wondered why the dancing cigars were so sad. We did not do the last two shows that Friday. But we worked all day Saturday and all day Sunday.

The TV was on Sunday morning and, as we were putting on our makeup for the first show, we witnessed to our horror Lee Harvey Oswald being shot. On Monday, the day of Kennedy's funeral, Radio City Music Hall was closed.

After our last show on Sunday night, I ran to Port Authority and boarded a bus for Washington D.C. When I got off the bus a policeman told me that the line to the Capitol Rotunda, where the President's coffin was on display for the public, was twelve blocks long.

I will never forget the young couples holding little babies waiting in the bone-chilling, freezing cold night.

Now, I have to go back in my story. Many movie stars and politicians are subject to receiving crank mail, and the Rockettes are no exception. We received some very strange mail that was postmarked November 9, 1963 from San Francisco, California. Addressed to the smallest Rockette, it arrived in a large 8 ½″ x 11 ½″ yellow envelope, and inside were many 8 ½″ x 11″ pieces of white paper upon which was printing and pictures cut out of magazines. The pictures were glued on the paper and there was nonsensical printing describing each image. There were pictures of Governor Nelson Rockefeller taken on his ranch in Venezuela. There was a picture of Fidel Castro, and a drawing of a flag with a star on it, maybe representing the Lone Star State of Texas. It was all very childlike, but very strange.

There was also writing of a $3 million proving ground for the Rockettes, and all in all it just rambled on and on and none of us could make much sense out of it. Center of the line Rockette Marcia Fiala shrugged her shoulders and said, "It sounds like an assassination attempt." The envelope and its crazy contents were tossed up on the grey metal shelves that housed our TV set along with many magazines and was forgotten about–until one Saturday morning.

Perhaps a week or so after Kennedy's assassination, I was making my bed. Charlotte Bullard, a Rockette from Boston was staying with me. All of a sudden I remembered that yellow envelope and shrieked to Charlotte, "Jesus Christ, I've got to get to the theatre!" I ran out of the apartment and went as fast as I could to the 51st St. stage door. I found the envelope right where it had been tossed and, as girls came in at call time, we were studying its contents. We gave it to our assistant dance captain, Violet Holmes, who was a little hesitant about giving it to Duffey, our captain. Ultimately, she did give it to Duffey, who in turn handed it over to stage manager Frank Hawkins. Frank told Duffey, "Don't let any of the girls touch it–fingerprints." Well, the envelope had already traveled across the United States from San Francisco.

The next weekend found me going out to Brooklyn after the last show and staying with Patty DeCarlo. Patty sat cross-legged on her bed in her baby-doll pajamas and got goose pimples on her legs as I related the story of the envelope and not being able to find Larry Arnold when I went to Washington, which left me frustrated. I needed a friend in Washington. With little chance of making it into the Rotunda before it was closed to the public, I had boarded a bus to go back to New York. My bones needed thawing and I watched the funeral on TV from the warmth of my living room.

Discussing the situation of the envelope with Patty, we both decided that I should contact the FBI to determine if they had indeed received the envelope. We also decided that I should speak to no one but J. Edgar Hoover. First, I called and asked to speak to Hoover. Needless to say, I did not get through to Hoover. So "agent ponytail on the end" went to the FBI. Barbara Douglas accompanied me. Barbara explained to the agent that even if this had nothing to do with the assassination of President Kennedy, which in all likelihood it did not, she was sure that the FBI would be interested in knowing about such insane information.

A week or so later I went back to the FBI by myself, detailing my information regarding the man I had met at President Kennedy's birthday party. My youth (I was a young twenty-two) and my imagination were questioning a perplexing situation. It got to the point where the FBI agent said to me, "Hey Ann, if you have any more stories for us, come back and see us, will ya?"

On my week off I went home to Boston and my dad came over to my mother's house where I told my parents all about it. Shocked and concerned for the welfare of their daughter, they said, "Oh, Ann, no, no, no; do you want to get involved?" My mom sighed, "I'm surprised you didn't ask to speak to J. Edgar Hoover."

"I did," I said.

"Oh Jesus," she cried, "What did you say?"

I said, "Hello, is Mr. Hoover there?'"

Mom carried on, exclaiming, "You're the same little girl as when you were trying to catch Willie Sutton." Notorious bank robber, Willie Sutton, pulled a fast one on a Brinks truck in Boston when I was a kid. A huge heist, my best friend Diane Brown and I decided that we would catch Willy Sutton. After going to the post office, located in Burrows & Sanborn Department Store on Union Street in downtown Lynn with my mom, I had spotted the poster "Wanted - Willie Sutton" and the $10,000 reward. I filled Diane in and she and I decided we were going to catch Willie. We looked through the phone book and started calling everyone named Sutton and casually asked, "Is Willie there?" Naively thinking we'd catch someone off-guard, who would say, "Hold on please; he's right here." I had to pay for the phone bill!

I do not write about the Kennedy assassination to shed more light and insight into the murder. Lord knows, that's been done again and again and again. But while we were kicking at the Music Hall, tragic history was being made. It struck my generation to the core. This was something that happened in history books, not in our lifetime, we thought.

When word got around backstage of my Washington escapades, head stage manager Hal Turner said of my going to Washington that Sunday night, "That was a very noble thing to do." My mother said, "That was a very stupid thing to do."

On that infamous Friday evening, the day the President was killed, when our last two shows of the day were cancelled, Bill Greenblatt, who worked in the publicity department at the Music Hall, took his girlfriend

Charlotte Bullard and me to the Manhattan Hotel on Eighth Avenue for cocktails. We rehashed and rehashed, and drank and drank. Our questions and the turmoil of a nation in trouble would continue through the decade with the murder of the Negro spiritual leader, Dr. Martin Luther King, and the murder of Senator Robert Francis Kennedy.

The sixties may have been a swingin' decade but, in actuality, the questions, the whys, the why nots, the how could this happen, and the why, why, whys were blowin' in the wind, but not necessarily the answers.

"I believe that this nation should commit itself to achieving the goal, before the decade is out, of landing a man on the moon and returning him safely to the earth. No single space project . . . will be more exciting or more impressive to mankind, or more important . . . and none will be so difficult or expensive to accomplish . . . "– President John F. Kennedy, Special Joint Session of Congress, 25 May 1961.

On November 9, 1965, I made my New York City singing debut. I should have gone to the moon. It was the Music Hall dinner break, which was between the second and third shows. That put the dinner break somewhere between 4:00 and 6:00 p.m. Some of us were sitting in the dressing room talking and playing a Johnny Mathis record. Suddenly, at 5:31 p.m., the record sounded warped, and then the lights went out. We were in total darkness as some of the Rockettes were shrieking. All we had were little inky-dinky birthday candles for when someone had a birthday. I asked if anyone had a transistor radio. We found one and when we put it on, the radio disc-jockey said the power failure extended to Staten Island. However, after running down the stairs to the stage, where I figured they'd know more about what was happening, I learned that this power failure extended to 75 miles north of Toronto and it affected much of the northeast.

The audience was in total darkness as the film went out. Organist Richard Leibert went out to the console and played the Mighty Wurlitzer. Bit by bit, the musicians were coming back from their dinner break. There was just enough auxiliary power to get the pit elevator up to performance level. The musicians formed a Dixieland band to entertain and pacify the audience.

As I was sitting on the pinrail, Warren Jenkins, head of the Sound Department, approached me and said, "You sing; you go out there and sing." Panic-stricken, I raced up to the dressing room to get my music. I was so nervous, and Patty begged me not to go out there and sing. I was escorted out to the center of the orchestra pit, where they held a flashlight over my head while I sang "Too Marvelous for Words." My second selection was "Put the Blame on Mame." and I was shaking so badly, I forgot the words. (Later on I wanted to put the blame on Con Edison.) After exiting and having a good cry on the pinrail, to my amazement Warren Jenkins sent me out there to sing again! This time I did a special material song about Rockefeller Center. It had some dialogue in it that got me a laugh when I said, "If this doesn't get me a raise, nothing will." Unfortunately, in the dark, it was difficult for the pianist, Ray Viola, to read the music. Carol Lawrence had sung this song on a TV special we did with her, and I learned the lyrics because my brother, Billy, had taped the show. Stagehand, Sal Lemac, went out and sang, too, and did an excellent job. I ran into his wife at street floor as I was running up and down the stairs, and told her, "Sal's onstage." She said, "I know; he's singing." I was devastated. Here I thought the Red Chinese or the Russians were going to bomb us, but I was the bomb.

While I was warming up on stage by the pinrail the next day, Russell came up to me and kidded me, "You're not going to get a star on your dressing room just because you went out and sang last night." "Oh, Russell," I sobbed, "it was terrible. Warren Jenkins sent me out there to sing and I came offstage and cried. And then he sent me out there again to sing!" Russell said, "And then you went out and sang "I Cried For You (Now It's Your Turn To Cry Over Me)", didn't you?" I was miserable. I wanted to sue Con Edison for damages. Dick Leibert said, "They're going to sue you for maligning the public."

The blackout was the talk of the towns and cities all over the northeast. I don't recall the exact cause of the power failure, but probably overload was the reason. In his nightly monologue on the Tonight Show, Johnny Carson hit on it when he said, "I told them they couldn't run an extension cord from Manhattan to New Jersey."

The poster department's Fred Eusini, a very nice man affectionately called Uncle Freddy by the Rockettes, was driving home during the blackout and picked up people who needed transportation. He told me he went to help the elderly and those who looked as though they needed help. Uncle Freddy was a sweetheart and a trooper. And so, the lights came back on and things went back to normal, or what passed for normal.

The decade was rapidly approaching an end and coinciding with the Apollo 10 exploratory mission to the moon, I did finally go to the moon. It was the spring of 1969. The show was the Daily News Show, a Leon Leonidoff production. "Dateline - Daily News" had sets by James Stewart Morcom, costumes designed by Frank Spencer and beautifully created by Leanne Mitchell and Penny Eugenides and those spinning seamstresses of the wardrobe department. Our hats were created by Andy Pellicano, and the Associate Producer was Nicholas Daks. Vocal arrangements were done by Will Irwin, with special lyrics by Albert Stillman. Emilia Sherman was Associate Director of the Rockettes and she did the choreography for our routine in this show.

Counter-end of the line Rockette, Joyce Hector Dwyer and I made a lunar landing, beating Neil Armstrong and

Buzz Aldrin to the moon. Two actors have never had such direction from a director.

"Shildren, shildren, I vant you to valk the vay they're going to valk on the moon," Leon directed.

"They don't know how they're going to walk on the moon," we protested. "They haven't landed yet."

Before we donned our astronaut costumes that weighed nine pounds each, we spent the week rehearsing in our leotards, trying to get used to the rigging and the rigors of flying. Our flying apparatus was courtesy of Peter Foy, the English Company that always does flying gigs. Our frayed nerves getting the best of us, Joyce and I went across 51st Street to Schraffts with the crazy Britisher in charge of the flying gear. He calmed us down somewhat by saying, "Either the cotter pin is in or it isn't." This was in reference to the harness we wore around our waists.

One night Louise Thompson and a couple of other Rockettes came down on stage to see how we were doing. Joyce told them, "The harness is hurting me in the shoulders, but it's hurting Ann in the crotch." They burst out laughing. Solemnly I replied, "I fail to see anything funny about that." "No, Ann, it's not funny, "they said as more laughter ensued. The harness was also hurting me in the armpits, causing me to wear Kotex pads under each armpit. This also caused more laughter when I put on my space suit.

The moon segment was called "Flash - Destination Moon" and was accompanied by a film from the National Aeronautics and Space Administration (NASA). In fact, Leon had been calling NASA all week to get ideas for the landing. Imagine, a Russian calling NASA! With Leon's thick Russian accent, perhaps it raised a few eyebrows, anyway. Also added into the mix was animation by Grumman Aircraft Engineering Corporation.

On that nervous opening day in June of 1969, the rocket ship took off with a blast-off effect created by gunpowder and CO_2 and the steam curtain. The lunar module descended and Joyce and I made our way to our respective ladders (there were two ladders on our LEM) to carefully descend the ladder and step carefully and cautiously onto the lunar surface (the stage), whereupon we were immediately hoisted up into the air.

Joyce was on stage right (prompt) and I was on stage left (OP). So when we hit our marks (a dotted line we were supposed to be on), the stage manager would give the cue to the fly floor for us to rise up into the lunar air. Joyce was clearly visible to the stage manager, but I wasn't. Consequently, if we weren't in perfect alignment with the dotted line, we would fly out over number three elevator, which was pre-set 14 feet below stage level. At dress rehearsal, Joyce, flying to OP side, went out like a pendulum and went down about 12 feet over the empty space. Standing in the wings, Duffey let out a scream in unison with Joyce's shriek.

The reason the third elevator was down was that our moon had people on it–the Music Hall Ballet Company. When elevator number three came up, the ballet company went into a crazy, sexy lunar ballet with choreography by Ronnie Lewis. It was an extremely sexy ballet by Music Hall standards, and had Armstrong and Aldrin been on this moon, there might be a lunar colony today inhabited by lunarinas! Joyce and I always survived out trips to the moon to return to earth and join the 34 other Rockettes for our number.

Actually, in this production the Rockette routine "Centerfold," with choreography by Emilia Sherman, preceded our lunar landing. Again, a stage elevator (this time number one) was pre-set 9 feet 10 inches below stage level, with the line of 36 waiting for the musical cue and the rising of the elevator. It is quite a theatrical effect to see the Rockettes rise up in a straight line from the depths to stage level. As we were standing and warming up below, up there, downstage on the wood was a group of young men from Florida. They were musicians who called themselves "The Impact of Brass." Behind these boys was a backfold, a very lightweight curtain. On their very last note, one of these young men, Doug Smith, was doing a gesture and looked up and fell through the backfold and down the 9 feet 10 inches. He landed on his coxa. Standing on prompt end, I saw this fall out of the corner of my eye, and ran over to him. Though he had landed on his back, he somehow rolled over and I was patting and soothing him as though he were a puppy and kept telling him he was going to be all right. Doug was shaking like a leaf blowing in the wind and managed to say, "I know, I know."

Tom brought the elevator up. They got Doug off stage on a stretcher, and then the elevator was lowered back down to the 9 feet 10 inch level, and then raised up again for our entrance. Again, in the tradition of "the show must go on," a few tear drops fell down the cheeks during this routine, too. Between shows I went to see Doug in the hospital. Hoping to cheer him up, this brave young man made me laugh. I said to Doug, "You know, you were a tough act to follow." He said, "Yah, nobody else wanted to go down." Apologetically, I said, "All I could think of when you fell was my junior high school course in First Aid and how I was supposed to put something over you to keep you from going into shock. But I didn't have much on me to take off." Doug quipped, "Well, you could have jumped on top of me." I concluded, "We haven't cried like that onstage since President Kennedy was killed."

There is a happy ending to this story, I'm glad to report. Doug married one of the Rockettes, Helene Grethlein, and they had twin boys and a daughter. Doug is fine and he and his wife live in Florida.

An Easter or two earlier than the Disney show, KLM Dutch Airlines flew in a troop of singers, one of whom had a day job as a tailor. A few Rockette eyebrows raised when the third floor elevator door to the dressing room opened and this Dutchman handed me my navy blue pleated skirt, which my father had bought for me when I was in the eighth grade and the styles of dress lengths were longer. Well, this Dutchman was one of Holland's finest tailors and he had shortened my skirt.

This show had a breath of spring fresh air about it, with the Rockettes wearing rose-colored Dutch-like costumes with a cute little white ruffle on the derrière, matching rose colored tap shoes, and blond wigs with the inverted ponytails slanting up, and a Dutch hat, white with rose trim. While we were tap dancing on the wood downstage behind the footlights, the number one elevator rose up about 2½ feet enabling us to back up a few steps and sit down on the elevator, where we did a little line-up in the sitting position. Tricky elevator moves occasionally made for interesting shows if there was a mechanical malfunction. Again produced by Leonidoff, this show began with the Glory of Easter Easter lilies, and concluded with the band car with the orchestra on it traveling upstage, and the entire company planting tulips on the pit elevator.

During the pre-Easter season of 1966, Radio City Music Hall closed for five days for repainting purposes, while we spent those five days upstairs in the rehearsal hall rehearsing for a television special. It was an NBC Special titled "Mary Martin at Eastertime with the Radio City Music Hall." Directed by Gower Champion, the taping involved three nights of working all night long. When our beloved creator and director Russell Markert announced that we would be doing this TV show he said, "Kids, we're gong to be doing a TV spectacular with Mary Martin. Gower Champion will direct. Now, now, don't get too excited. This is going to involve a lot of work, a lot of hard work. I want you kids to get a lot of rest. I mean it; this is going to be difficult. Now, is there anyone here who does not wish to do this show?" Not a creature was stirring; not even a mouse.

Three hundred men worked around the clock in eight hour shifts on a huge scaffolding in the auditorium, while the Ballet Company, Choral Ensemble and the Rockettes rehearsed six hours a day. We worked two days before Miss Martin's arrival. When Miss Martin walked into the rehearsal hall and saw the 90-person cast Mr. Champion had staged, and this did not include the orchestra that was placed center stage, she asked Champion, "You mean you're going to fit all this in that little box?" She was referring to what is known as the TV set.

We were placed in triangular formation with singers in one group, ballet in another group, and the Rockettes in a triangle. Mr. Champion would walk through each group, viewing each group through the eyes of an imaginary camera. Fortunately for me, I was one of the lucky ones. As I mentioned earlier, the theatre was closed for five days during our rehearsal period, but the Music Hall show itself, opened on a Saturday, unlike its usual Thursday opening day. I was on my week off for the Saturday Music Hall opening, but the poor girls who had to do both the Music Hall opening, which meant a 7:00 or 7:30 a.m. Saturday dress rehearsal, plus four shows per day Saturday, Sunday and Monday, also had to do the all-night taping.

At approximately 10:30 p.m. on the Monday evening following the Saturday opening at the Music Hall, we were bused out to Brooklyn to the NBC Color Studios. Arriving at NBC Studios that first night, we taped the Glory of Easter Pageant. The cement floor of the studio, almost the size of a football field, was spray-painted a deep blue and bright red. Circling this tremendously large oval-shaped studio were white curtains. The lights, camera, action routine started around the stroke of midnight and it was a wrap at around 6:00 a.m.

After the four daily shows at the Music Hall, on Tuesday evening the bus was waiting for us at the 51st Street stage door. This time the cement floor had been repainted a luscious lavender and everyone (Miss Martin, Ballet, Singers and Rockettes) was costumed in white. Even the musicians wore white dinner jackets. This night we were taping our opening number. The music was Jerry Herman's "Put On Your Sunday Clothes" from the Tony-award-winning "Hello Dolly," which Mr. Champion had also directed.

A rather intricate taping night, it involved what was called "stop tape," which meant that at certain intervals the cameras would stop rolling for a few seconds and we all had to run beneath the cameras eyes to get placed in a new and different location. This night we wrapped at 7:00 a.m.

Each night the NBC staff had sandwiches and coffee prepared for us and, of course, each of us had to go to hair and makeup. The NBC makeup department supplied us with little plastic clear boxes that contained a luscious pink, creamy lipstick. We also were given pancake makeup and a pink rouge designed for television lights and cameras. The makeup was spring bright and very flattering on everyone. Television makeup was different from stage makeup. For live theatre we would wear dark red lipstick, a darker pancake base and red rouge. However, years later, when Bob Jani came to Radio City, he wanted a more natural look in makeup on stage.

At the assigned time, each girl sat in a makeup chair similar to a dentist's chair, where NBC makeup artists expertly made up each Rockette. Then we moved onto hair. I had put gargantuan rollers in my hair; the hair stylist took my curled hair and in minutes swept it up into a smashing up-do. Emily Sherman laughed and said, "There goes your Cleopatra hairdo, Ann." It was amazing how quickly the hair stylists did each girl's hairdo, and every hairstyle was unique. Since this TV Special involved three days of taping, I finally gave in and bought a hair dryer because I knew I would need to shampoo my hair perhaps twice daily and set it and have it dry quickly. I'd never used a hairdryer, even in winter; nor did I use hairspray, but I gave in on the hairspray, too.

Wednesday night was our last evening of taping and also proved to be our most difficult night. This night we taped the Rockette routine and were dancing on a bright canary-yellow cement floor (not too good for the legs that cement). In fact, while standing around waiting for the cameras to start rolling, I could see all the veins in everyone's legs. At 5:00 a.m. the Rockette routine was yet to be "in the can." We all knew the song "Three O'Clock In the Morning-we danced the whole night through," but never took it seriously until then. Everyone had a laugh when Rockette Paulette Harris remarked, "Mother, I'm doing this for you."

We were placed in a diagonal line and Miss Martin introduced each Rockette individually, according to the state from which she hailed. This was tricky since it was set to music with Miss Martin's opening line, "This is something I've wanted to do for a long time." Frustrated with the length of time it was taking she said, "This is something I've wanted to do for the past two hours." Finally, the introductions and the Rockette routine were done and the bus was waiting for us at 8:30 a.m. to take us back to the Music Hall. However, Mr. Champion asked six of us to stay to re-tape a military tap kick lineup with Miss Martin. Mary was placed in the center of the line and, since she was not too tall, the shorter girls, of which I was one, were placed on either side of her.

Mr. Champion promised us that we would be driven back to the city in two limousines in time to do our Music Hall show. Now, I was one of the poor girls who had to do both the taping and the show opening on the Great Stage, after my week off. Finally, finally, finally, that kick lineup was finished and we quickly put on our street clothes and then waited and waited for the two limos at the stage door. This wait prompted Carol Albro, affectionately known as "Stick" (she wasn't skinny; she had a beautiful figure) to quip, "Maybe they're going to send the (NBC) Peacock and we're going to fly back."

At 9:45 a.m. Thursday morning we walked into the Radio City stage door, went up to the dressing room, crawled into our sleeping bags, and before we could finish a dream, awakened to the familiar voice heard over the public address system four, and sometimes five times a day, "Twenty minutes to overture, stand by, please: twenty minutes to overture, stand by." Doing both this TV Special and the regular show at the Music Hall was exceptionally exhausting on everyone; but with every Music Hall opening, exhaustion was the name of the game.

Since my husband Tom had a "key job" in that he was the control board operator, he was responsible for the gymnastics of the contour curtain, the intricate moves of the four stage elevators, the revolving of the turntable, the opening and closing of the footlights, and the bleeding of the steam curtain in preparation for a steam effect, etc. This was all done under the direction of the Stage Manager, the captain of the stage, and it was nearly always done in accordance with a musical cue.

On a dress rehearsal morning, Tom's call was often at 3:30 or 4:00 a.m. for lighting rehearsal. Other stage hands had been there the entire night before, striking one set before putting up another; and mind you, they had already worked all day on the outgoing show. Often on a dress rehearsal morning I would arrive with coffee and egg sandwiches to find stagehands draped across curtains, sound asleep.

Speaking of sleeping, an unusual circumstance in a Russell Markert show had the Rockettes going on at the beginning of the show. We usually went on towards the end of the show. This show had a Japanese theme and we wore short little red and gold brocade kimonos, with a beige body-stocking underneath and a black wig-hat fashioned to look like the beautifully coiffured black up-do styles worn by Japanese women. Since we had twenty minutes or so between the Rockette routine and the finale, at which time I was supposed to be one of three girls in three separate gondolas going around on the turntable, I would slip off my kimono and crawl into my sleeping bag to catch twenty winks. One fine night, my dressing room alley mates, Patty DeCarlo, Darlene Whalley and others walked right over my sleeping bag and my sleeping body and went down to the finale without me. They were talking and didn't notice me as they stepped over my body. When Violet Holmes, who was captain at the time, came up to the dressing room and found me curled up in my sleeping bag, she asked, "Ann, aren't you in the finale?"

"Yeah, is it time?" "Don't' bother," she said. "Why didn't they wake me up?" I asked. "I don't know how they could do that." "I don't either," my captain said.

A captain and/or a co-captain always went out front to catch our routine, and gave us any necessary notes. So there was an empty gondola going round and round on the turntable. Even worse–no one missed me, until Violet found me on the dressing room floor.

Posing for the line-up picture was also an opening day ordeal. Standing on one leg with the other raised in a "front passé" position, 36 girls would try to balance and remain smiling while photographer Henry Rapisoda would be out in the house yelling, "Hold it, hold it, hold it, hold it, HOLD IT! "Ah, life upon the wicked stage ain't nothin' what a girl supposes."

One early morning I had inadvertently crossed union lines. On the bus ride home the night before, Tom and I talked about his not getting a call for the rehearsal the next morning. He was needed to close the footlights (otherwise, we couldn't do the big wheel), among other things. Since girls came in from Long Island, New Jersey and other far distances, I called Tom at home and asked him how to close the footlights, rather than not have the rehearsal. This rehearsal was known as a holdover rehearsal, and when girls came back from their week off, a girl might be placed in a different place in line. Hence the need for a rehearsal. I got into a bit of trouble over that with one of Tom's bosses. What did he think; I was trying to take my husband's job?

Tom's control board was so intricate that it even intrigued Frank Sinatra. In the early eighties, Mr. Sinatra was doing a benefit for the American Cancer Society at the Music Hall. The President of Rockefeller Center, Alton Marshall, and the Director of Stage Operations, John Henry Jackson, were sitting on the pinrail (by the ropes that pulled many of the curtains) when Sinatra came down onstage in preparation for his concert. Mr. Jackson called Frank over to the pinrail to introduce him to Marshall. Sinatra was cordial enough, shook Marshall's hand and then made a bee line for Tom, who was standing by the control board, which looked like the dials on a submarine. Sinatra directed and shouted to Tom, "Dive, Dive, Dive!"

At this time in religious history, the Polish Pope John Paul had just taken over the Papacy. My husband said to Frank Sinatra, "Hey Frank, have you heard the latest? Hail Mary, full of grace; now the Italians are in second place!" Frank laughed and said, "Oh, I'll guess there'll be a lot of these."

When Frank was rehearsing for his concert, we were rehearsing up in the rehearsal hall for a special two night concert of our own. The star was Peter Allen, the extremely talented Australian songwriter who was also a first-class entertainer. Wow, could he dance and sing and throw himself up and all around the piano! He practically jumped inside the keys. He was wonderful.

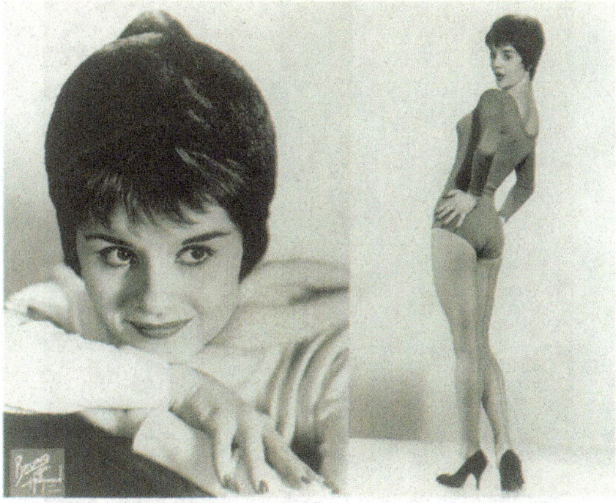

My first professional picture photographed by Bruno of Hollywood -1960. I was nineteen.

"Peace on Earth
Good Will Toward Men
Let's Make This World a Safe
Place for each Girl and Boy
and if only all the Soldiers
in the World were made of Toy"

The above message was the introduction to the Rockette routine. The Parade Of The Wooden Soldiers, the first time I did it. I always loved the message and asked Russell for permission to use it on my Christmas card.

Photo by Tom St. John

Tom at the Control Board with Lassie.

ALL THAT JAZZ -1976
photo by Vito Torelli

Surrounded by Rockettes Lt. Governor Mary Anne Krupsak kicks up a leg. All Press cameras were on us until the Concord flew overhead. Then all cameras aimed skyward. We were on City Hall steps in our efforts to save the Music Hall. 1978

Mickey Mouse and me 1962
from the author's personal collection

photo by Alden Seth
1965

1966

1976

Emily Sherman once referred to the above costume as our repertory costumes. Note: The changes the costume department made over the years

Brazilian number
1960

Taking off for the moon
1969

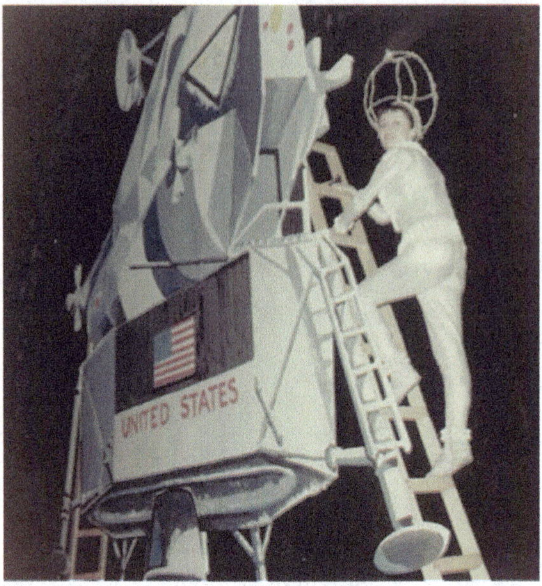

A soft lunar landing. Our lunar module had two ladders.

Clowning around between shows: I decided to try to develop my own clown makeup.
1976

When we got back into the dressing room after our rehearsal ended for the day, we could hear Frank over the PA system. I said to Pam Kelleher, "Pam, let's go down on stage and go out into the house. With all the security they may not let us out there, but let's see how far we get." We did and we got out into the house. This was absolutely thrilling to watch Ol' Blue Eyes in his baseball cap, rehearsing on the pit elevator. Singing in his casual, melodic style, Sinatra crooned "Angel Eyes" and between notes took a puff on his cigarette and immediately sang the next word. "ANGEL EYES-that ole devil sent:- they grow un-bear-a-bly" (puff-exhale) "bright."

Since this was a benefit for the American Cancer Society, I said to Pam, "Frank is puffing on a ciggy; I don't think the Surgeon General is going to like this."

During a break, Peter Allen ran up onto the pit elevator to say hello to Frank. Frank said, "Peter, this is such a great room for you." A 100 foot proscenium and Frank says it's "a great room." Anyway, cigarette and all, Mr. Sinatra's performance at the Music Hall was a smashing success.

Another camel story comes to mind. During the run of the Christmas show, Peter Allen and the RCMH production staff were having a meeting, trying to figure out a new entrance. You always have to have a great entrance. Somebody jokingly said, "We've got a camel; why don't you come out on a camel?" Peter astonishingly asked, "You've got a camel?" And so, the "I Go To Rio" entrance was on camelback. Again, I was side-stepping my way in front of a camel to the off-beat of claves and wild percussion, not only with the Music Hall Symphony Orchestra in the pit, but with Peter's own orchestra on stage.

What a night! The house was packed with mink-coated celebrities. It might have been a cold February night, but it was hot inside the Music Hall. Peter's show, which was to have been on three different nights, was so exciting that they decided to bring it back for a return engagement three weeks later.

The opening number of Peter Allen's show involved the Rockettes coming up on the #1 elevator dressed in white top hats and tails, carrying classic Fred Astaire canes. The backdrop was NEW YORK in bright lights and, of course, our tap number was to "I Love New York." Upon completion of our routine, the star of the evening, Peter Allen, descended on number two elevator to thunderous applause. For a couple of hours, Peter absolutely held that audience in the palm of his hands.

A great guy and an outstanding entertainer, songwriter, singer and dancer, Peter was one of those rare personalities who was not only extremely talented, but extremely nice. Whether back-bending over the piano stool or riding a camel, Peter Allen was a consummate entertainer.

As I am writing this book, we are all saddened and mourning the death of ABC-TV news anchorman Peter Jennings. With élan and precision, Mr. Jennings brought us World News Nightly, and when disaster struck, he was known to be on the air for sixty hours. At the age of 67, Peter Jennings succumbed to lung cancer. As a tribute to and in honor of Peter Jennings, allow me to address the conflicts that cigarette smoking created in the dressing room.

Both of my parents smoked, but neither my brother nor I ever did. Like Mr. Jennings, my pretty mother also succumbed to lung cancer the day before her 67th birthday. The lovely ballerina, Nora Kaye, of the American Ballet Theatre also died of lung cancer around the age of 67. One of my favorite teachers at Lynn English High School was Mary Ishkanian. She was wonderful to me and used to take me into Boston to the theatre. One evening we went to the ballet and saw Nora Kaye dance. After the theatre we went for a bite to eat at Steuben's (the Sardi's of Boston) on Boylston Street. I got all excited when Nora

Kaye and her party walked in and were seated in the booth next to us. But I was shocked when Miss Kaye lit up a cigarette.

However, Miss Kaye was not the only dancer who smoked. When I got into the Rockettes, many of the girls were cigarette smokers. It used to drive me crazy, and at one point drove me out of the dressing room and into the hallway to put on my makeup. I was on the you-know-what list (the letter falling between R and T among the smokers). Russell and Emily used to tell a story of a ballet girl at the Roxy who was smoking in costume and the costume caught on fire. She died; the flames spread so rapidly she could not be saved.

When we would take the passenger elevator from the seventh floor rehearsal hall to the third floor dressing room, cigarette smokers would light up, but they would be unable to smoke because the elevator was so crowded. They had to stand with one arm up in the air holding the cigarette, like the Statue of Liberty holding her torch. Then finally, the non-smokers became more vocal. When we went on tour to Lake Tahoe, we had a smoking and a non-smoking dressing room. I always knew when I had a smoker next to me in the line. After the kick lineup, while in the final pose waiting for the applause, the smoking Rockette would not regain her breath as fast as a non-smoker.

All I can wish for is for all you cigarette smokers to wake up some morning and absolutely hate cigarettes. As for you dancers, singers, actors, and everyone else, if you haven't started to smoke - try not to be seduced by peer pressure. For all you girls who want to stay young, Cigarettes are an estrogen suppressant. Please don't smoke. You'll feel better, you'll dance better, you'll sing better, and you'll breathe better.

One of my all-time favorite routines, if not the number one favorite, was the Cowboy number. It was in a beautifully simple, neat Russell Markert production and it illustrated the contrast between the oriental East and the occidental West. The show opened in the Far East with the ballet girls dressed in two-piece costumes: a bra midriff and a long flowing skirt cascading around the stage, and using finger symbols. This ballet featured the wonderful Beatrice Kraft who, by the way, when she first rehearsed with the orchestra was so out of breath because she'd been smoking three packs of cigarettes a day. She managed to increase her endurance and danced an exciting number to Khachaturian music. Mid-show, it segued to the West with a saloon and barroom scene and, of course, a barroom brawl, complete with chairs and bottles being broken over cowboy heads; and then the Rockettes entered to the theme music from the epic film "The Big Country." Russell and Emily had heard the music on the radio on WPAT, a Patterson, New Jersey station that played mostly classical music. It inspired them to choreograph this classic western routine.

Wearing white tight-fitting trousers that had splotches of black sequins, Dalmatian style, and brightly colored satin blouses of various colors, black sequined gaters over tap shoes that looked like boots, and cowboy hats, we had the greatest steps to execute in this number. At one point the orchestra stopped playing and it was just the sounds of taps, which started off in a trot, graduated into a canter, and finally a gallop before the music rejoined us for the kick lineup. I never, ever tired of doing this routine; I just loved it. A very simple, but beautiful and romantic finale consisted of a lone cowboy and cowgirl walking arm in arm upstage into the sunset.

Another great Russell routine (there were so many) was "Shakin' The Blues Away." We wore tangerine-colored costumes, which had a skirt with a slit up the side and was all fringe that could shake the blues away. Sexy and full of bumps and grinds, Tina Gorgano joked. "My ovaries are going to the second balcony."

This routine was a sizzler and at one matinee, when a passage had been cut, we went right into a mid-routine kick lineup unbeknownst to Evelyn Ray, who hadn't been told about the cut. Evelyn quickly and expertly joined us kicking, while asking those of us around her, "Is there anything else I don't know?"

In February of 1962, Russell again produced the stage show, which was "Rhythm de Paris." Accompanied by the film "A Majority of One" starring Rosalind Russell and Alec Guinness, the Rockettes performed a Can-Can and a great Can-Can c'était. Joined by the ballet girls in costumes matching ours for the finale, we wore dust rose-colored Can-Can dresses with white ruffled petticoats and white ruffled bloomers over black tights. Trudy Carson forgot her bloomers in one show, so we had one black bottom out there amongst a semi-circle of white ruffled bloomers.

The Corp de Ballet augmented the Rockettes in another routine, "The Blue March," a very girly, sexy march to "I Love a Parade." And we reciprocated by assisting the Ballet with "Rhapsody In Blue," Ravel's "Bolero," and the Undersea Ballet.

One evening before the fourth show, Duffey came into the dressing room and announced that some of us would be participating in the ballet number of an upcoming production. She read off the names of the girls augmenting the ballet, and told them, "You're going to make trees. So, you thought only God could make a tree."

Rhapsody was done on the turntable surface only. It had a chrome plate mounted on the top of it and the chrome was placed on an angle. Consequently, it was a mirrored effect. We wore silver and blue long gowns with a slit up the side, showing pink-tighted legs. Downstage-left was a white concert grand piano with soloist Anthony Makas striking the keys of the Baldwin. At a certain musical point, the turntable would revolve and, because the chrome plate was pitched on an angle, the dancers felt as though they were dancing uphill, and revolving. The

Ballet Company, the Rockettes and two soloists, a man and a woman, did all their dancing on that 43-foot diameter turntable.

A friend of my mother, Pat Caggiano, who became the Mayor of Lynn, always took me to dinner when he came to New York. Arriving in New York one time with a buddy of his, Ace Capola, the two men took me to Toots Shor's restaurant between shows. Happily eating away my calves liver and bacon, Pat looked at me quite seriously and said, "You know, I wouldn't have said this at the beginning of this meal, but you've got a good appetite. Geez Ace, I'd rather buy her a mink coat than feed her for a week."

On another visit to New York, Pat brought a young Boston University drama student with him. At the time, we were doing Ravel's "Bolero" which began with one person center stage, then two, then three, four, etc., until there were close to a hundred for the climax of the number. Again we went to Toots Shor's and as we were sitting down, the young man said to me, "You know, Ravel had the sex act in mind when he wrote 'Bolero.' I'm not embarrassing you, am I?" "Oh no, no," I, red-faced, assured him. This was a summer show and the film was "The Music Man," which had a good long summer run. When I got back to the dressing room I announced, "Guess what kids, Ravel had the sex act in mind when he wrote 'Bolero'!" Always ready with a bright quip, Patty DeCarlo put her legs up on the dressing room table, crossed her arms and exclaimed, "Well, just think, we've been having sex for twelve weeks and we didn't even know it!"

Performed behind a scrim, the Undersea Ballet required the services of the Peter Foy flying company again, since there were swimmers who would "swim" through the air, though appearing to be under the sea. All of the sea creatures were dressed in bright, vibrantly colored costumes. Four ballet girls were sea horses, and they flew, er swam. Center sea, a clam shell opened up and an adagio couple, Ron and Joy Holiday, came out of the shell. They wore very skimpy costumes, with Joy in a bra and bikini panties and Ron in a bikini; and they had silver body paint all over their bodies—head to toe—including their costumes. Ron had actually patented this silver paint, which they had on all day.

Ron and Joy came from Old Orchard Beach, Maine and they were a thrilling couple to watch. Combining acrobatics and ballet, Joy would balance en pointe on top of Ron's head. While warming up in the wings one day, Ron was holding Joy high above his head. Joy was in a split position. Ron joked, "She's got the stiffest crotch in the business."

When not performing at Radio City, Ron and Joy played nightclubs across the country and throughout the world. Ron decided to add a panther, a black leopard, to the act. The big cat wore a diamond collar to match one that Joy wore. We were in the rehearsal hall one day while Ron and Joy were rehearsing with the big cat and we could see the spots underneath the black fur of the animal.

Years later I heard on TV that Ron had a Bengal tiger in the act. He also had a thirty-five year old man assisting him. The tiger attacked and killed the young man. Both Ron and the parents of the deceased man decided not to put the tiger down, but unfortunately, sometime later, tragically, the tiger also lunged at Joy's throat and killed her. Ron and Joy were a sweet couple, a very nice twosome, who brought their balletic, acrobatic adagio to the theatre adding grace to everything they did. The were graceful both onstage and off.

The lead swimmer in the Undersea Ballet wore two wires going up the side from each hip, instead of the usual one that goes straight up the center back, in which case the flyer is in a vertical position. Wearing two wires enabled Patsy Turner, wife of head stage manager Hal Turner, to do flips and pirouettes between the two wires. Patsy performed this beautifully and was one of the most graceful fish in the sea. The rest of us portrayed a variety of sea creatures. I was the third amoeba next to the second paramecium on the left.

At rehearsal, ballet mistress Betina Rosay was trying to figure out how to get Neptune's Chariot off the stage. Asking herself and others, "Now how do I get rid of that damn chariot?" Giggler Janine Frasier said, "Five thousand guppies swim on and take it off." Visually colorful and beautiful, the Undersea Ballet was very alluring and captivating- guppies, amoebae, paramecium and all.

There were so many wonderful and beautifully creative Rockette routines over the years. The Sailor routine, the Cowboy number, Cindy Lou, Six Flats Unfurnished and I Enjoy Being a Girl, Shakin' the Blues, Romanza del Caribe, The Blue March, The West Point March, The Parade of the Wooden Soldiers, The French Maid, The Can Can, The Slick Chick routine, The Doll Dance, The Dutch number, Kalanoit, Beauty and the Beat, Fiddle Faddle, Faruka, Vamps, and so many others. I don't think Russell really got all the credit he so deserved for his innovative dance routines; and Emily, too, who was such an asset to Russell, and then came into her own as choreographer when Russell retired.

Still dancing and kicking his leg way up over his head at age seventy-two, Russell used to say, "I hope you girls can still do this when you're my age."

A very strong and clear sounding tap dancer, Emily would work the troops hard. Sometimes known as General Sherman, she could be a task master.

When Mary Ann Strilka, sister of Romayne, married concert master Jesse Cusimano, they arranged to be married at St. Malachy's Church on 49th Street so we would all attend the wedding. Unfortunately, it was opening day and we were doing the West Point March. Emily rehearsed us between the dress rehearsal and the first show, so most of us could not make the wedding. As for the West Point March, it was flawless.

Counting took all the pleasure out of dancing for me. However, there are times when counting is absolutely necessary. Four routines that come to mind are: THE TOY SOLDIER, THE WEST POINT MARCH, THE COWBOY NUMBER, and Benny Goodman's IN THE MOOD.

Any march where you're going from opening up the gates (two lines of eighteen opening in parallel lines to one another) going to a six spoke wheel, or the big wheel, requires mental concentration and counting.

If you're familiar with the melody of STARS & STRIPES FOREVER, try counting to the melody 13,14,15,16,17,18,etc. It goes against the nature of a 5678 beat.

For THE WEST POINT MARCH we had to march in a straight vertical line (all 36) from the audience's view point, from stage right to stage left --27 together, about face, wait two counts, and 13 together into center stage to prepare for the big wheel.

Itchy costumes were another problem, especially in the summer, or for that matter in the winter, when the heat was on full blast. Lamé costumes, sparkly, but, oh, so itchy, were very irritating. If one does not like the costume, psychologically it could make one not like the routine.

Once a week costumes were sent out to the cleaners and when they came back, most particularly the Wooden Soldier jackets, would burn the girls' skin under the arms. Some of the girls' armpits would get all red because of the cleaning fluid and the Wooden Soldier trousers were so stiffly starched they could stand upright on the floor all by themselves!

Erratic tempos made for nervous taps and painful kicks. A good kicking tempo was hard to come by with the three different conductors we had in the old days. Raymond Paige, Leon Zawisha, and John Dosso commanded the baton and there were times when we didn't know what to expect.

A good kicking tempo is comfortable-- not too fast where one is unable to get one leg up in the air and down again in enough time to get the other leg up and back down, and not too slow where the dancer feels she has to sustain the kick in midair.

During the early sixties, Marc Platt, a former dancer with the Ballet Russe de Monte Carlo and one of the brothers in Seven Brides for Seven Brothers, came to the Music Hall to be choreographer and director of its Corps de Ballet. Along with changing the corps name to Ballet Company, Marc created some very unique and interesting ballets. During his first show in February, 1962, The Kennedy Administration was in full swing and there had been much publicity about the President's bad back, and how his doctor, Dr. Janet Travell, had recommended he use a rocking chair. So, Marc Platt had the thirty-six of us begin our routine in thirty-six hot-pink rocking chairs rocking to "Old Rockin' Chair's Got Me." We slid out of the chairs and into a smashing number created by Russell to the Ray Coniff arrangement of "It Was Just One of Those Things." The film of the program starred Rock Hudson and Doris Day in "Lover Come Back."

Wearing black and white (half and half, like the cookie) sequined toreador pants, part of a one-piece outfit, we went immediately into the finale. We–Rockettes and Ballet girls–were downstage of a white picture sheet, so our shadows were forecast on the screen. One day Marc said to me, "I can always tell it's you in the finale. Know why?" I got all excited thinking he was going to tell me about my dancing. "Because your ponytail bounces up and down and I can see it on the screen."

Before one Marc Platt production, about five of us were on our week off, so we were available for a flight out to Flint, Michigan. The flight was courtesy of General Motors and we went to the GM Proving Grounds to shoot some film that was to be used in the up-and-coming Marc Platt production. The theme of that show was sports car racing.

Marc did a great many ballets for the Ballet Company. One really cute one had a backdrop of a spider web. The female star fly was caught in the web but, alas, was rescued from the villain spider by the male super fly. The ballet also incorporated a fly police force, and when they marched on with a huge spray can, it brought down the house. The fly police force carried billyclubs, too. They were very Mac Sennettish, just a silly riot to watch.

The decade was rapidly coming to a close. We had lived through the Cuban Missile Crisis, with Duffey announcing, "In the event of an attack, we will report to the large rehearsal hall. That means when the bomb hits, it hits us first." We were going to get that routine right, no matter what.

We had also seen the assassinations of a President, a Negro Spiritual Leader, and a United States Senator. Marilyn Monroe and Judy Garland had died. We had witnessed the lunar landing. And in 1967 we had gone on strike. Gone was P.J. Moriarty's, where we had the Equity discount menu with Prime Ribs of Beef for $2.05; the 99-cent first show of the day was a thing of the past, and we hoped that the turbulence of the sixties would be gone, too.

Chapter 4

THE 1970s ...
LAST CALL; STAND BY, PLEASE
LAST CALL; STAND BY

In the seventies, the houses began to dwindle. The swinging sixties had changed America, and the audiences changed, too. Radio City Music Hall always had an agreement with motion picture studios that any film that played the Music Hall would not be shown in any other movie house within a 50 mile radius of Radio City. The Music Hall was a family-oriented theatre, and the taste buds of the American public wanted something more. If we had a family film, we would be asked, "Why don't you have something for adults?" And if the choice of the film had a more adult content, we'd hear, "This isn't good for children." I used to do the telephone recordings for the Music Hall, announcing the name of the film, the stars, the stage show theme, and the times of the shows. I would record for Monday through Friday, and then Saturday and Sunday. One night I was recording and the telephone operator received a call from a man in Georgia. He was flying up to New York City with his kids and wanted to know what the "short" was; he already knew the feature film.

Audiences have a tendency to congregate towards the center section, so the end girls in the line would be playing to empty seats. New girls coming into the troop wouldn't know what it was like to play to a capacity house. And with this downward spiral came our first hiatus. It spanned from mid-January into February, 1974–a three week lay-off period.

Working at Radio City Music Hall may have been a grind, but on the positive side, it was about the only job in show business where one worked fifty-two weeks a year. As Evelyn Ray used to say, "I came here looking for steady work and I've been working steadily ever since."

There was that time when the price of a ticket was 99-cents before noon, one of the best bargains in New York City. Before noon, this price included a movie and a stage show. Again, on the plus side, we started to travel, playing Lake Tahoe, Las Vegas and London. Performing elsewhere brought renewed vigor to everyone.

Christmas of 1970 brought a Leonidoff production called "Cheers." The film was "Scrooge," starring Albert Finney and Alec Guinness. Barbara Ann Cittadino, the girl who rode up in the Otis elevator with Tanya the elephant, her trainer, and me, had a solo part playing a little girl named Laurrine, who joins the Rockette line.

At the ripe old age of twenty-nine, I finally got my driver's license and, as chance would have it, I, too, had a part in a crazy automobile act. Mr. Leonidoff had seen this act in Las Vegas and wanted to do his version of it in New York. He commissioned a couple of men, Dino Rogers and Klaus Ansorge from Las Vegas, and me. We drove a mock automobile in front of a picture sheet showing a film shot in London, where they drive on the opposite side of the road. We were busy Christmas shoppers and it looked as though everything we did was bass-ackwards. Wouldn't you know that during the run of this show I got my drivers license! Thanks to Tom, who rented a car and took me over to Riverside Drive to practice parallel parking, I managed to get my license on the first try. But, I'm still not a very good parallel parker.

Sophia Loren put in a personal appearance at the Music Hall while doing a press conference when her film "Sunflower" opened in the fall of 1970. Stuck in midtown traffic, she and her husband Carlo Ponti abandoned their car somewhere on 50th Street and walked to the Music Hall. In a rush, she wanted to check her makeup. Tom gallantly handed her a mirror he kept backstage. He also kept Miss Loren's finger prints on that mirror for eons.

Tom also offered his hot-pink stool that he kept by the control board to Diana Ross. From then on, the hot-pink stool was known as the Diana Ross stool. When we did a television special in 1978 with Ann Margaret, Gregory Peck, Alan King and Beverly Sills, Ann Margaret would sit in a chair by the control board and Tom would massage her feet. Tom did all right. This TV special was a Christmas special, and we had a camel named Henry. There was a sign on the mirror by the quick-change room: "Henry loves Bubbles," the nickname for the lovely Beverly Sills.

In July, 1971 we had a new choreographer make his entrance to the Music Hall. A veteran of the Broadway stage and film, Peter Gennaro came into the Hall as producer, as well as choreographing for us. His first number for the Rockettes was a tribute to Charles Lindbergh. We danced to "Lucky Lindy" and wore airplanes—actual miniature Wright Whirlwind 225-horsepower, 9 cylinder radial engine planes—if you can imagine this. Their wing span was approximately three feet. Our costumes were that silver-grey aeronautical look with flight caps with goggles, and silver tap shoes with big silver bows à la Busby Berkley.

We did a false exit to get out of the planes and made a re-entrance doing inside fan kicks from prompt to OP. My fellow astronaut, Joyce Dwyer, had to do all the kicks all the way to OP. I told her one day that that was definitely an unfair division of labor. I don't know, or at least, I hope there isn't as much traffic on a runway as there was in the wings hopping out of those airplanes. This was traffic with a capital-T, with no control tower!

That previous summer, Tom and I took a six-week vacation and got married in Fairbanks, Alaska. We made 27 trips going downstairs out of my apartment to pack the car and the first night out we got as far as Eastern Pennsylvania - car trouble. Bad news, since we had a limited amount of days to meet our boat (aka motor vessel) in Prince Rupert, British Columbia. But, we made it; and we made it back to RCMH where, from then on we'd take the #7 bus home together after the last show.

The lay-off periods increased, not only in number, but in the amount of the duration of the time off. This was new for us. It wasn't like being in a Broadway show, where it closed and the next morning one had to go out auditioning again for another show. At the Music Hall, when one show closed, the very next day a new show opened.

In late January of 1976, however, we were set to play Harrah's at Lake Tahoe, Nevada. This was the first time the Rockettes had been away from home since 1937, when they had sailed for Paris on the Ile de France for the Paris Exposition, where they received France's highest honor, the Grand Prix of the Republic. On Friday, January 23rd, a 0-degree Fahrenheit day in New York, we boarded United Air Lines DC-8, flight 35 for San Francisco, California where we did some preliminary publicity. Put together by the Edgewood Travel Agency, our itinerary looked like this:

Arrive at San Francisco	- 12:30 p.m.
Press photo in Cable Car	- 1:30–2:00 p.m.
Bus to Fisherman's Wharf	- 2:00 p.m.
Press Luncheon	- 2:45–4:45 p.m.
Bus Tour en route to Airport	- 5:00 p.m.
Arrive at Airport	- 6:00 p.m.
Depart for Reno, Nevada	- 6:40 p.m.

There were photographers located at strategic spots throughout the city, as we rode the cable car around that city by the Bay. We lunched on filet of sole, green beans, spumoni, cocktails and coffee, and, of course, sourdough bread at Scopa's on Fisherman's Wharf. Afterward, a bus took us across the Golden Gate Bridge before we departed San Francisco for the 30-minute flight to Reno.

Pam Kelleher, who had gone out to San Francisco earlier to do some radio shows, rejoined us for the last leg of the trip to Nevada. Pam sat by the window, Carol Toman was in the middle and I was on the aisle. Both Pam and I had a fear of flying. In fact, Father J. P. Sullivan of Holy Innocents Church in Pleasantville NY, who used to come along with us to our local watering hole, wrote a prayer for Pam and me called the "The Pam Ann Prayer to Overcome the Fear of Flying." We took it with us every time we flew. Pam and I braced ourselves in the forward position - ready for take-off. Carol took one look at us and said, "Will you two sit back? You look like a couple of jockeys on a horse."

The three of us decided to order a scotch after the flight attendant told us we must order immediately due to the short duration of the flight. Upon going into her purse to search for her wallet, Pam discovered that it wasn't there. She didn't leave her heart in San Francisco; she left her wallet. With her mind on her wallet, Pam forgot about her fear of flying. Fortunately, the wallet was found at Scopa's restaurant with everything intact, and it took its own flight to Reno. Because it was snowing in the Reno area, our flight was in a holding pattern, but we finally landed. After an hour's bus drive from Reno, we arrived at the Lake Tahoe Inn after 9:00 p.m., Pacific time.

John Henry Jackson produced and directed our out-of-town show and brought some ballet girls and singers along, besides the thirty of us Rockettes with him. John also brought with him one of the very best adagio acts in the business, Francois Szony and Rita Agnese.

Thanks to the kind heart of John, our dress rehearsal that opening day did not begin until noon. It could have been an 8:00 a.m. call, but the night before, we all went to see Frank Sinatra's closing show. We also did a publicity photo with Frank before his last show. Needless to say, Frank's show was great. It was a sophomoric thing to do, but Pam, Carol and I tracked Frank down at the Hideaway Lounge, a very lovely and quiet cocktail lounge. Sinatra liked to go there, and I can understand why. Beautifully lit with tiny lights on branches of trees, this lounge was indeed a hideaway. What a great night. Joan Peer struggled to get to the photo shoot. Sick as could be with the flu, how many times in one's life does one get to do a photo shoot with the Chairman of the Board?

Because of Joan's illness, Harrah's decided to bring two more Rockettes in from New York as swings. Originally, they would pay only for thirty girls, but soon realized that at least one swing, and probably two, was essential, since opening night we opened with only twenty-nine girls. The program read "Harrah's Lake Tahoe presents Kicks 76 Featuring the World Famous Rockettes from Radio City Music Hall, Produced and Directed by John H. Jackson." The orchestra was under the direction of Brian Farnon, and the Rockettes did a Bicentennial Salute with choreography by Peter Gennaro. Sets were by John William Keck, costumes by Frank Spencer, special music and lyrics by Don Smith, musical arrangement by Richard Hayman; our Stage Manager was Chuck Gilette, costumes executed by Leanne Mitchell, electronic fireworks by Mobilcolor Corporation, wigs by Venicelon, and special screens by Mel Hurley Company.

During the weekdays, we were on our own, but on the weekends we did a different show and opened for Wayne Newton, Bill Cosby, Merle Haggard, Neil Sedaka, Charlie Rich and Sammy Davis, Jr. Bill Harrah always offered his guest star a cottage on the lake or the penthouse at the Lake Tahoe Inn. Sammy chose the penthouse and had a great party for us there. He was such a nice man and so down to earth. While helping myself to some food along the table line, Sammy happened to be next to me. I said, "Mr. Davis," to which he corrected me and said, "It's Sam."

I reminded him that the last time I'd seen him was on a telethon he had done for the National Safety Driving Commission. Penny Singleton, then President of AGVA (American Guild of Variety Artists), our union, had called the dressing room and asked me to take up a collection and bring some of the girls over to the TV station. When we got there, Mr. Davis, Sam, said to me, "Oh, you're the one with the loot. Will you make a speech?"

"Oh, thank you for remembering it," Sammy said.

"Thank you for remembering it? I'll never forget it!" I said.

Since the Music Hall was closed during this time frame, Tom was on hiatus; and since he was a train buff, he took the train across the country to join us in Lake Tahoe. He helped stage manager Chuck Gillette time the show, and rented a motel room for us. So I had two motel rooms–one at the Lake Tahoe Inn, where I roomed with Dottie Belle Meymann, and the one with Tom at a cute little place called Doc's Cottage–which was on the Nevada side of the street. We got a kick out of the Nevada snow plows pushing the snow back to the California side of the street.

Since Tahoe is higher in altitude than the mile-high city of Denver, Colorado, we were cautioned about the altitude and the effect it could have on us. In fact, there was an oxygen mask backstage. One Rockette used it just to try it; another one really needed it. But after a few shows we had built up our endurance.

The whole company was invited to Bill Harrah's home for a lovely lunch. Nine limousines (eight owned by Harrah's, one rented) picked us up at our Lake Tahoe Inn. There were five Rolls Royces and four Lincoln Continentals. Tom, Chuck Gillette, Holly Jones, Dottie Belle, Francois Szony and I were in the first limousine.

The exterior of Harrah's house was a faded grayish-brown wood, and when Tom rang the doorbell, none other than Bill Harrah himself opened the door and welcomed us into his magnificent home. Magnificent may not be a big enough adjective to describe his home, which was deceiving on the outside, since it was so much grander on the inside.

We walked in through a foyer that immediately sprawled out into a huge living room—about five living rooms' worth, I would say. On the right was a spiral staircase that led to a downstairs level. There were no windows on the front-door side of the house, but there were massive windows on the backside of the house—wall to wall windows, I mean, the whole wall consisted of windows. And that whole wall encompassed the entire back side of the house, both upstairs and downstairs. The view looked out onto beautiful Lake Tahoe, which at the time, looked like a rolling ocean. A heated swimming pool was neatly shelved in an upper jutting-out patio. The deck was approximately 20 feet down and towards the windowless side of the house, in the center of this huge room, was an enclosed area that housed a bar and some beautiful crystal.

To the right of the living room among living rooms was a raised fireplace. We had a group picture taken with Bill and his wife Verna Harrah. Cocktails and hors d'oeuvres were served and then somehow some of us latched on to a tour given by tour guide Bill Harrah himself again. The color scheme throughout the whole house was beige, orange and brown—earth colors—and very masculine, with these gargantuan windows overlooking Lake Tahoe.

Mr. Harrah took us to the cellar (cellar hell, it was an engine room, clean as a whistle). With large red steam pipes, like most engine rooms on a submarine, it was immaculate. I expected Frank Sinatra to jump out any minute and yell, "Dive, dive, dive!"

After returning to upstairs to finish our cocktails and hors d'oeuvres, we then proceeded downstairs again to the magnificent dining room, where there were two very long rectangular tables paralleling each other. And I mean these tables were long. There were fifty-six of us, and Mr. Harrah invited guests of his own, so there were probably seventy guests for lunch. While dining, we enjoyed that majestic view of Lake Tahoe.

We were served a lovely salad with Italian dressing, rolls and butter, and for the entrée very tender beef and green snap beans with bacon and mushrooms. No potatoes. This was a be kind to chorus girls' special. Although, there was a dessert of a tortoni-type of cookie and raspberry sherbet. Red wine was served with the meal and empty glasses were constantly filled. It was an absolutely delicious lunch and we couldn't believe that we were the guests of this lovely man. Tom was seated next to Mr. Harrah and said he enjoyed his conversation with him immensely. Soft spoken with a kind and gentle manner, Bill Harrah was always so kind to the performers who performed at his showroom. It was indeed an honor and a pleasure to have been a part of the entertainment in the South Shore Room at Harrah's Lake Tahoe.

Entertainment manager, Bob McClure, took us on a tour to the star's quarters between the 16th and 17th floors at Harrah's. A long hallway took us into the star's suite. Again, a massive living room that was very modern and had a long, circular, cream-colored leather couch. There were two extremely large matching chairs. In fact, two people could sit in each chair at the same time.

On the far right of the room, away from the windows, was a well-stocked bar, and over the fireplace a figure-printed carved wall. Press a button and down came a movie screen for 16 mm films, tapes, stereo, the whole bit. A cream-colored shag rug covered the floor. In the left corner of the room stood a walnut baby grand piano.

There were three or four bathrooms and stairs that led to an upper level, where the kitchen contained a well-stocked freezer, a Corning Ware oven, and a dining area with a table with a marble top. Downstairs had a master bedroom with his-and-her bathrooms.

Our month's stay at Harrah's flew by quickly. We had the best of both worlds there, I think, a natural setting with beautiful pine trees surrounding a lake, not to be believed; and a casino at night alive with show business. California on one side, and Nevada on the other; who could ask for anything more?

The Harrah's people were wonderful to us; they could not have been nicer. They were so warm and friendly and made our stay so comfortable. And, of course, Bill Harrah certainly lived up to his reputation for treating his show people employees to nothing but the best. We were not only lucky and fortunate to have had this gig, but to have known this wonderful man, Bill Harrah.

Rumor had it that since we had played Lake Tahoe, could Las Vegas be on the agenda? Negotiations were in the works. Meanwhile, we went back to Radio City and opened the Easter show. Two months later, we were segueing from spring to summer and the Country was preparing to celebrate its Bicentennial.

On June 17, 1976 we opened with "Celebrate 76," produced, directed, and choreographed by Peter Gennaro. The overture was "Listen To the March" and the Purdue University Marching Band had everyone stepping in time to "March to the Music." The Rockettes were a "Red, White and Blue Rainbow" with Violet's choreography. And a beautiful Japanese dancer named Kuniko Norai narrated via dance a brilliantly choreographed piece by Peter depicting our nation's history through dance. It traced America's evolution with dance starting with the Minuet, the Castle Walk (with a cute couple depicting Vernon and Irene Castle), the Charleston, the Black Bottom, the Lindy, the Jitterbug, all the way up to Rock.

The next production was produced by John H. Jackson. It was a French circus show called "La Fantasie du Cirque," in which we wore black turkey feathered headdresses and ponytail of black turkey feathers on the derrière. We did some prances with eighteen Rockettes coming out on each side, meeting in the middle, and proceeding upstage to loop through a big ring, the way tigers and lions do in the circus.

I was the lead girl going upstage on my side, and the heel of my tap shoe caught on the bottom rung of the ring. I had cleared it, falling upstage of it, but ended up on my bottom, falling right on top of my ankle. It hurt like hell and I couldn't move. Now, there's a traffic jam behind me with girls prancing in place. Barbara Boho Moore and Terry Spano picked me up under the armpits and literally carried me off into the wings, cautioning me not to step on that foot. Within seconds my ankle swelled like a ball.

Carol and Pam took me to Roosevelt Hospital. They waited as long as they could before leaving for the next show. But not before some drunk, who kept poking his head into the room while the doctor was examining came out to the waiting area and announced to the girls, "Ah, isst busted." I had torn the anterial ligaments in my ankle and was forced to take some time off for a few weeks.

With each passing day, the Las Vegas trip was seeming like a reality. Finally, the official word came. We were going to be the opening act for Glen Campbell at the Las Vegas Hilton. On October 3rd, 1976, we all met at the 51st Street stage door and were bused to Kennedy Airport.

With a couple of scotches to fortify us, and Father Sullivan's Pam Ann Prayer, we were up and away on TWA flight 191. We stopped in cloudy and rainy Phoenix to refuel before arriving in Las Vegas. As we were descending, Carol was cracking up the other passengers. She had the headset on and kept repeating, "Phoenix, come in; Phoenix, come in. I'm not reading you. Come in Phoenix. Hello, hello."

The following are little excerpts from my journal of our Las Vegas debut.

10/04/76 - Reported to Hilton Showroom for an 11:00 a.m. rehearsal. Centralized air-conditioning - Freezing! Because of Hoover Dam, Las Vegas can turn the air conditioner on HIGH. Ladies, forget about décolletage and a cocktail dress for the showroom. You'll freeze! Had only one hour rehearsal before they broke for lunch. Musicians weren't called until 1:00 p.m. Orchestra sounded great, but usual tempo trouble.

10/05/76–Opening Day. Two shows a night - 8:00 p.m. and midnight. First show was disastrous because of tempos. Dottie Belle Meymann was my roommate. Our room was on the 22nd floor and was all done in red. There was a beautiful view of Las Vegas and we could look down on the marquee: GLEN CAMPBELL and THE ROCKETTES.

Again Tom was able to get away and come out to Las Vegas via train, his favorite mode of transportation, and he rented a little apartment for us. Two homes again - incredible. The night before the opening we had caught the Hallelujah Hollywood show at the MGM Grand. We were surprised and delighted to see Tanya, the elephant in the show. After the show, we looked up Jenda Smaha, who invited us to his home. It was great to see Jenda again and everyone got a kick out of his walking through the casino with Tanya, who would stop and play the slot machines with her trunk. (By the way, this was not the same Tanya who played the Music Hall. She was a different elephant.)

10/06/76–Change in the show - wore white costumes - more show-girly. Then had an 8-minute change into red "All That Jazz" costume. We were the opening act for Glen Campbell. His act was approximately fifty minutes. Then we came on for the finale.

10/07/76–Glen does not like the fact that we close the show. We'll do opening number in the red "All That Jazz" and then segue right away into the "All That Jazz" routine. Finale - we'll do the drum number. Have 8 ½ minutes to change, but everyone is worried because we have to put on white tights, trunks, change of bra, white blouse, gaters, tap shoes (from red to silver), a Jacket, a wig and a hat. Good news - we don't have to wait around the fifty minutes for Glen to finish his act. So, we'll have more time between shows. We'll be able to see other shows on the strip. A blessing in disguise.

10/8/76–Today I went bottomless in Las Vegas. In New York I had purchased a Rudi Gernreich bathing suit, the Thong. God knows I couldn't wear it in the Commonwealth of Massachusetts or New York. If I was going to wear it at all, it had to be in Las Vegas. And I did.. I had arranged with Joe, the lifeguard, to secure a whole bunch of pool chaises that one uses in the water, so that Tom could shoot pictures of the Rockettes reclining in a line-up in the chairs in the water. I thought it would make a cool billboard across the desert. But after a few photo shots, a water fight erupted. There goes the billboard in the desert wind. However, the Rudi Gernreich bathing suit was the headliner at the pool that day. Joe said to me, "Murph, that suit was built for speed." In the afternoon Dottie Belle, Jerry Bailey, Tom and I took a drive to Hoover Dam.

10/11/76–Tom and I drove Carol and Cathy Beatty, daughter of ex-Rockette Claire Beatty and her Music Hall musician husband Norman Beatty, who played a beautiful trumpet, to the town of Beatty, Nevada and the Toiyake National Park. Back at the ranch at the Music Hall, it was fun to listen in on Cathy's telephone conversations. She'd have her mom on the outside phone and her dad on the PAX (Private Address Exchange house phone) and she'd say to her dad, "Mom wants to know what you want for supper." That evening, a friend of mine, Frank McBrien, the chief projectionist for MGM, caught our show. Frank's son-in-law is Bill Hampton, a famous western artist who painted nudes, Indians and horses.

10/15/76–Today was another wonderful day with dinner at Rena and Jenda Smaha's house. In the living room there was spread out on the floor a huge polar bear skin rug that Jenda had purchased from a gambler who was down on his luck. He had paid $1,200.00 for it. Draped over the couch was a leopard skin, which Jenda had shot himself. The atmosphere was a combination of the North and/or South Pole and Africa. The kitchen was of the ultra-modern variety, just off another living room. In the den/living room, where we sat and drank, were two fish tanks and a cage with two parakeets. There was also a huge stone fireplace with white elephant head statues on either side of it, and a tremendous TV. The entire house was exquisitely furnished in a perfect harmony of man living with his animal friends.

In the backyard four baby chicks resided in a children's plastic swimming pool. Older relatives of the chicks had killed one, so Jenda moved them into the pool. Two large dogs then escorted us around to the back, where we met the laying hens. Jenda said one of the dogs had killed about fifteen of them, so he put some wire up in the fencing that would shock the dog.

We reminisced about seeing them when Jenda, Rena and Tanya worked Circus Circus. Rena assisted in the act and she looked stunning in a bright red sequined gown. She wore her dark black hair in an up-do, and with her lily white skin she was a beauty. Rena had a girlfriend in town, who had been president of Elvis Presley's fan club at one time, and she stood in line at the International Hotel (later renamed the Las Vegas Hilton) to get six tickets for Elvis's show.

I'll never forget how many beautiful girls went gaga over Elvis and just wanted to get as close to him as they could. The opening act was so loud that Tom had put Kleenex in his ears. As Elvis was singing "You Ain't Nothin' But a Hound Dog." we all happened to turn around to look at Tom. He was sound asleep. Las Vegas can be exhausting.

Next we visited Villa Tanya, where the two elephants resided. The working Tanya was four years old and had been working for two years. The younger elephant was two years old and still in training. Each elephant was chained to a station; otherwise, the older one would bite the younger one's tail. Jenda showed us an example of the training routine. He put a drum in front of the elephant and handed her a drumstick, while Jenda counted rhythmically 1-2-3-4, 1-2-3-4, 1-2-3-4. I asked if Tanya responded to applause. He said "No," but maybe on stage with lights and people, and after getting used to performing, she might respond.

In the barn there was a medicine cabinet for the elephants, and Jenda had built an overhead shelter that had a sprinkler system, so they could shower. Jenda said he had paid $10,000 for the baby elephant. He won't be able to get anymore, though, because of the Endangered Species Act.

On an acre of land, the whole spread was surrounded by a white wall. But what a spread it was. Of course, the pièce de résistance of all were Jenda and Rena's children. Gina, 12, is a dark haired beauty and Christian, an adorable blue-eyed blond. A precious and sensitive little boy, we had fun at the end of our visit by running through the spraying garden hose.

Saturday, 10/16/76 –We picked up Susan Boron at the Hilton at 1:00 p.m. and headed for Boulder City to visit with ex-Rockette Viva Reynolds, now married to musician Tom Pastor. Between shows, Tom and I cabbed downtown to Fremont Street and caught a show at the Golden Nugget. Wow, small world! We knew two kids in the show: Robert Rayo, a former Music Hall ballet boy with whom I had studied tap, and Pat Wilkins, who had been in the Music Hall Ballet Company. The show was "Frederic Apcar presents Colonel Zachariah's World Renown

Genuine Wild West Extravaganza" with choreography by Ron Lewis. It was an excellent little package-only an hour in length, but a very entertaining show with excellent dancing.

Because everything is so close together there, downtown Las Vegas really sparkles with the millions and millions of twinkling bright lights. It almost made Broadway look anemic because of so much glitter.

10/17/76-Thanks to Tom Pastor, Barbara Ann Cittadino, Sue Boron, Tom and I sat in the wings and caught the Lou Rawls show between our shows.

10/18/76-Took some pictures of billboards. On one side was a really sexy drawing of a girl in black garter belt and stockings; on the other side of the billboard was a picture of Glen Campbell and The Rockettes.

10/19/76-Early day; up at 9:30 a.m. At 11:30 a.m. drive to Hilton to pick up Jerry Bailey Arsburger, Helene Grethlein Smith (future mother of twins) and Katy Braff. This was our longest voyage of the season—291 miles in all—to Death Valley. We reached the Furnace Creek Inn, where there was a cluster of National Park-style buildings. We all went into a coffee shop for milk shakes and burgers. Usual tourist stuff; bought postcards, etc. Everything was hunky-dory until that moment, when we were ready to leave. We were all in the car and Tom poked his head in the door and said, "There's an imminent disaster."

"What?" we asked.

"I put my jacket in the trunk, and the keys are in my jacket."

We froze for about one second. It was now 3:30 p.m. and we had left Las Vegas at 11:30 a.m. Our stage call was 7:30 p.m. and we had over a hundred miles to travel! Everyone jumped out of the car, running in every direction. Jerry ran into the coffee shop and exclaimed, "Is there a locksmith in the house? This is an emergency." Where do you find a locksmith in the middle of Death

Valley? Well, there was one there. A young man who worked around the place ran off some distance looking for him on the golf course. I think the locksmith was on the ninth hole when this kid caught up with him.

Finally, after what seemed an eternity, a car pulled up with the man in it. We all asked anxiously, "Are you the locksmith?"

"Yep," he proudly said. I practically kissed him. A macho guy, he walked up to the car with the attitude of "if anyone can do this, I can."

Katy had figured there was nothing she could do, so she went off to the museum. I nervously asked Tom, "How could you do this to us?" Because we were going to see Raquel Welch that night, I had my hair set in pink curlers. Pink curlers in my hair and gold loop drop earrings in my ears.

Mr. Macho Locksmith was picking the lock when Tom appeared at the back of the car and said, "I can open the trunk."

"How?" we asked.

"I have the key to the trunk right here."

The expression on the face of the locksmith was not to be believed. I went into my rain dance, jumping up and down with my pink curlers and my gold loop earrings bobbing. Just at that moment Katy came out of the museum and asked, "What's the matter, Ann?"

"He found it; he found it," I said, jumping all the while.

Tom had opened the doors of the car to let the hot air out. He had his jacket on and asked himself, "Well, what do I need this for? I'll put it in the trunk." And he did. He had put the car key in the white bag that held the camera, which was up front, under the driver's seat.

The locksmith put his tools away. Tom gave him a couple of bucks for his trouble, and offered the young man who'd fetched him some money, too. Jerry said, "Please come out and see our show. You will be our guest; we'll get you in."

"No thanks," he said. "I'm never leaving Death Valley."

We hopped into the car and mercifully went on our way as everyone looked on at these crazy show people. That place will remember u,s. They'll probably say, "Remember those Rickets?" Maybe they'll even erect a historical landmark to us, we joked–a historical, hysterical landmark. We laughed all the way back to Las Vegas.

That evening, Tom looked as though he was surrounded by a harem at Caesar's Palace, where we saw the Raquel Welch show. Eleven Rockettes and Tom enjoyed Raquel's opening act, David Brenner; and of course, Raquel was gorgeous and surrounded herself with four boy dancers.

10/20/76–It was cloudy when we woke up this morning, but the sun came out later, so I decided to go to the pool. I also made another decision–to wear my thong. When I got to the pool and got set up with a lounge chair, I sat down and started to undress. I had my blouse off and some of the kids asked, "Ann, what bathing suit do you have on?" I smiled, they smiled, and they knew. As I took off my jeans and my cheeks hung out, I remarked, "You know, you have to have balls to do this." Meanwhile, Joe, in his lifeguard hut, was taking in the whole scene, also with a smile.

I sunbathed for a while. Gee, it was good to sit on the cheeks. I was getting hot, so I decided to go into the pool. Had a good dip. Joe reiterated, "Hey Murph, that thing's built for speed." It was a great suit to swim in and after I was out of the water for five to ten minutes, Tom arrived. We took a bunch of pictures. Thank heavens a lot of other girls were in the pictures, too; people were sure looking.

During the last show tonight, when Glen Campbell's act began, Wayne Newton went out instead, and sang Glen's opening song "Gentle on My Mind." Roger Miller was out there, too. When I heard Wayne's voice singing, I dragged Tom back to the wings to watch. After a few songs, I went downstairs to get dressed. They were still going at it when I got back upstairs. Wayne and Roger finally finished and Glen was onstage alone. All the girls were standing in the wings. Tom said that Wayne had come through and greeted them all. I was sorry I had missed him. The girls had gone; Tom and I walked upstage and I stalled a little bit. Roger Miller was upstage talking to some people and along came Wayne. I walked up to him, introduced myself and extended my hand. He took it, bent down and kissed me–a long one. He was bending my false eyelash, but I didn't care. Wow!

Between shows we went to the Marina Hotel and caught another Ronnie Lewis show, "Bare Touch of Vegas." Good show, good dancers, and incredible costumes. In one number, the girls wore blue denim jackets and trousers with rhinestones around the jeans and red fox tails hanging from their sleeves and on their legs. The girls wore the denim jackets open and were bare breasted. The girl and boy soloists were great. The girl wore a beautiful rhinestone G-string.

10/21/76–Tom finally did it today; he locked the keys in the car, leaving them in the ignition. But he got a coat hanger and managed to get the car door open in seconds. Between shows we caught Bobbie Gentry's show at the Frontier Hotel, courtesy of Nels Hansen, a former Music Hall stagehand, now a Las Vegas transplant and a union representative for I.A.T.S.E. (International Alliance for Theatrical Stage Employees). Nel's mother and wife work in wardrobe and they all enjoy Las Vegas and its climate.

Friday, 10/22/76–It was cool and overcast when we woke up, so we decided to go on a trip. Tom called Katy around 11:00 a.m. and asked her if she could be ready by noon. She said she could be ready in a half-hour. Later, we called Sue Boron. Picked up the girls at noon, gassed up, and went on our way to the Valley of Fire and its huge red rock formations; just beautiful. Then we went to an arm of

Lake Mead and into a place for lunch that was full of flies. This was a fisherman's stop.

After the last show we went to the Silver Slipper and saw the star of the show, Irving Benson–old time Burlesque. Lost $2.00 worth of nickels in the slots. Oh well, this is Vegas.

Saturday, 10/23/76–Another thong day at the pool. Eileen Collins offered me $5.00 just to walk around the pool. I said I'd do it for $500! Met Henri J. Lewis, Executive Vice-President of the Las Vegas Hilton. Mr. Lewis offered me four free meals in the Imperial Crown Lounge (very expensive) if I gave him my bathing suit. "You don't know the way I eat," I said.

He said, "That's all right."

I thanked him for the nice letters he had sent us. He seemed pleased, and asked if we were having a good time out here.

Regardless of the show production, whenever the passenger elevator would open on the dressing room floor of the Rockettes, stage manager George Cort, if he was on it, would yell out "Everyone on stage for the Hawaiian number!"
photo by Tom St. John

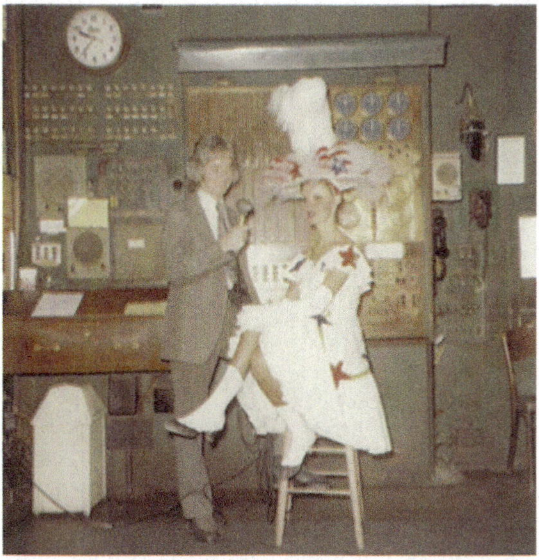

Former Everett, Massachusettes school teacher, stage manager Stephen Kelleher with his Rockette sister, Pam.
photo by Tom St.John

(l-r) Stephen, Pam, Shelia Rodriguez, Carol Toman, and Ann.
photo by Tom St. John

I visit the animals in the animal room---just off stage right.

LUCKY LINDY – AUGUST, 71

PETER GENNARO SHOW #1

Peter Gennaro's first RCMH show

We wore airplanes, dancing a tribute to Charles Lindbergh. We did a false exit to ditch the planes. It was really a sight to see 36 Rockettes stepping over 36 airplanes in the limited space in the wings, in order to make a fast re-entrance doing fan kicks.

In this John Jackson produced show we did a tribute to Charlie Chaplin, spelling out CHARLIE with our bamboo canes at the end of the routine.

The mini tour for The New York State Department of Commerce. United Airlines flew us to San Francisco, Braniff to Dallas, and Eastern to Miami-all in one week!

Poolside in Dallas, Texas - (r-l) Judy Little, Dee Dee Knapp, Eileen Collins, Carol Toman, Pam Kelleher, and me.

1976

We were the opening act for Glen Campbell. This was a great gig. We had so much time between shows we were able to see other shows on the strip.

Me poolside in the infamous bathing suit--Rudi Gernreich's "The Thong." If I couldn't wear it in Las Vegas, where could I wear it? It's now or never- or no where, I figured.

(l-r) Me in rollers, Jerry Bailey, Katy Braff, Helene Grethlein. This was our Death Valley trip. That night, between shows, we were going to see Raquel Welsh. Hence, my rollers.
all photos from the author's personal collection

"Oh, I'm just fabulous," I said. "We don't want to go home."

"Well, don't," he said.

Sunday, 10/24/76–Had two good swims today; wore the more subdued black net Fredericks of Hollywood bathing suit.

During the last show tonight, Eileen Collins came running over to me and asked if I had any pasties to which I replied, "No."

"Well," she said, "I'll have to go to Frederick's tomorrow, then." She then told me how she had pulled Terry Lindenthaler's bra down at the pool and everyone was laughing hysterically. So now, it seems there's a conspiracy to get Eileen. She wants to have pasties on under her suit. "For that matter," she said, "I'd better get a matching G-string, too." Tomorrow will be an interesting day at the pool.

Monday, 10/25/76–As it turned out, I didn't get to the pool today, but the event didn't take place anyway. When I got up this morning, I got on the phone and called a few jewelry shops. Finally, I found one that would make a gold disc with a swimmer on one side of it and an inscription on the other side saying, "TO JOE - LOVE, THE ROCKETTES - 1976." This will be for Joe, the lifeguard at the pool; he has been so nice to us.

We went over the Broadway shopping complex; we had to look for a sketch of a swimmer for the jeweler. Bought the book "JAWS" by Peter Benchley. Went home and had some lunch, and then headed to Hoover Dam, celebrating its 40th birthday tomorrow. This time we went down into the dam; very impressive and very huge. Sixteen thousand men built the dam and ninety-two of them died while building it. Today they take two thousand visitors a day on tours of the dam. It takes well over a minute for the elevator to descend; it goes down over 500 feet.

Between shows we went to the Baronshire Room and had prime ribs of beef. I love their salad; they prepare it in a chilled bowl right at your table.

Tuesday, 10/26/76–The north wind was blowing like mad today. I started to walk over to the pool and got over by the Las Vegas Convention Center and had to turn back to get the car. When I got to the pool, Katy Braff was leaving. I asked how it was. She just commented with, "Wait 'till you see it."

Well, I saw it all right. I was the only one there. The wind was blowing so hard that the water in the pool had waves; it looked like the ocean. When one of the lifeguards brought me a mat for the lounge, he nearly blew away with it. I never took off my clothes.

Meanwhile, Dee Dee was taking in the whole scene from her window and laughing. She had me paged to ask me for a weather report. In order to answer the page, I had to hand in the mat or it would have blown away. I went back to the lounge chair after answering the page, but only lasted a few more minutes.

After 2:00 o'clock we headed for Rena and Jenda's. Bought five T-bone steaks on the way. We went out into the backyard with Jenda while he fed the elephants. They had a great big bowl of oats and had had carrots for breakfast. And they have hay to munch on all day.

Rena and I had quite a talk while Jenda showed Tom some pictures of India and Ceylon. Rena told me about the Tanya I had known, and she started to cry when she told how Tanya had died. The elephant had outgrown the act and was sold to some people, but she developed hemolytic equali bacteria, an intestinal disorder. Humans can contact this disease, too, but on a human they can operate, on elephants they cannot. After dinner Rena sang for us, showing that she has a beautiful soprano voice.

Otto Baraccini's father, John, was there when we first arrived. A fascinating family, the Barricinis had a chimpanzee act. They also have a gorilla and an orangutan. We reminisced about their having played the Music Hall.

Time is going quickly now; Tom leaves on Thursday.

Wednesday, 10/27/76–After an Italian dinner at Leonardo's Tom watched the first show from the wings. We both hated to see the time come to an end; and yet, it will be good to get home, too.

Thursday, 10/28/76–D-Day, ugh! Tom was up early. Oh, how I hated to see this day arrive. This was our last morning seeing our little bird friends in our friendly little palm tree outside our window. We still had a lot of packing to do. We got my things over to the 22nd floor of the Hilton. Tom had a great idea; we ordered room service for lunch. Then the inevitable arrived. It was time for Tom to leave. I walked him down to the car and had a tearful, kissful good-bye.

The wardrobe ladies made us some delicious cake tonight. One was chocolate and the other had green frosting and walnuts. Both cakes were delicious. It's a good thing we do eye-high kicks a lot. After the last show I went with Carol and Pam to the discotheque lounge. Our disco dancing days were dwindling.

Friday, 10/29/76–Between shows tonight Carol, Pam, Susan Kingsland, Dee Dee Knapp, Linda Deacon, Helene Grethlein Smith and I went to see Ginger Rogers at the Desert Inn (affectionately known in Las Vegas as the DI). Miss Rogers had to be 65 at least. Well, her act is fabulous; actually fabulous isn't a good enough word to describe it. She danced and sang, backed by four good looking boys. Ginger is a doll, and she's so warm and friendly with her audience.

She introduced us from the audience with all the superlatives one could hope for. She did many of the numbers from her old movies. Reminiscing, she told the audience that she first starred on Broadway in "Girl Crazy," where she introduced that wonderful Gershwin song "Embraceable You." She ended her act fondly caressing a black top hat that one of the boy dancers brought out onto the stage. A spotlight focused on the hat and she said, "Good night, Fred."

We went backstage after the show. She was a warm and gracious as she could be. She kissed us all and posed for a picture with us. The energy that emanates from this woman is contagious. What a living doll! Needless to say, we were really in high spirits for our second show.

After our last show, Carol and Pam and I took a taxi to Caesar's Palace to see Steve Lawrence and Edie Gormé. Steve and Edie must have had 45 musicians. What a classy, stylish act. This fantastic twosome did a Cole Porter medley and, of course, Edie sang her latest hit from "A Chorus Line, Kiss the Day Good-bye (What We Did For Love)". We were so glad to have seen this show; it had been highly recommended by Tom Pastor.

After leaving Caesar's we went over to the MGM Grand and headed for the coffee shop. Carol called Picasso, the juggler in our show, and he joined us. We ordered breakfast and Picasso drove us all back to the Hilton. Got to bed around 5:00 a.m.

Sunday, 10/30/76–After last night's shenanigans I naturally woke up later than I wanted to. Didn't go to the pool this morning because I had to go to the Broadway Mall to pick up Joe's disc at noon. Met Carol, Pam and Picasso down in the coffee shop at 11:30 a.m. Picasso drove us to the Mall, but as Las Vegas luck would have it, the disc that was supposed to be ready by noon was not going to be ready until 3:00 p.m. Carol wanted to cancel the whole thing. "Oh no," I said, "I'll wait."

I went across the highway to the mall and Picasso drove Pam to Joseph Magnin's on the strip. Picasso and Carol said they'd try to come back for me, but didn't know if they would or not. I went out of my mind in this tremendous Broadway Shopping Mall. They had a pet store with animals all over the place. Also, there was a dog show in the center of the mall. I must have gone into fifteen stores.

Exhausted and scared (worried about the disc and the time), I crossed over the highway, back to Huntington Jewelers. The disc still wasn't ready, so I walked back outside and heard my name being paged. They'd come back for me and they had put the top down on the car. We all went into the jewelers and waited another moment or two for the finishing touches to be put on the disc. Well, it was beautiful, with the girl (from the Jaws book) swimming on the front and on the back the inscription to Joe: To Joe, Love, The Rockettes, 1976. We were all delighted with it, except for Picasso who shrugged his shoulders.

It was great driving back with the top down. Too bad we couldn't go to Lake Mead. Picasso let us off at the long entrance; Pam and Carol went to take a nap. I went up to my room and got dressed for the pool. It was about 3:30 p.m. before I got there, but I did have a good swim. Went up around 4:30, showered and got ready for tonight's party, which was given by Judy Little and Johnny Haig, head of many Vegas hotel orchestras.

The party was held in "The Clubhouse," a good sized dwelling that members of a condominium rent. It was a huge room with a fireplace in its center. Judy and John had rented a big silver piece that flowed with Cold Duck. A bartender served us all the drinks we wanted. For food, there was ham, cheese, salami, antipasto, ravioli, potato salad, macaroni salad, etc.

Viva and Tom came to the party. It was quite a party. At one point, some goblins arrived–people dressed up in Halloween costumes. Jerry Bailey brought her husband. Katy Braff brought her parents; they'd just flown in today. Katy's dad was eighty-four years old.

There was a smaller room off the large room that contained a pool table. I walked by and Carol T. was shooting like Minnesota Fats. She was playing with Joe Amata, our lifeguard.

Ina, our wardrobe lady, drove us back to the Hilton. We did, after all, have another show to do that night. Many of the kids were trying to cram everything in, as our time in Las Vegas was getting short. Some decided to stay up all night. Carol and Pam talked me into going to a new discotheque called the Brewery. It had just opened while we were there and was the "in" place to go. We got to bed at around 5:00 a.m. Dottie came in even later.

Sunday, 10/31/76–Woke up early, in spite of my disco night. This was the last day and everyone wanted to get to the pool early. I made some breakfast and went down to poolside at about 10:45 a.m. Had one good swim. At 12:30 p.m. I left the pool reluctantly, and went upstairs to shower and shampoo. Wouldn't you know, it was an absolutely beautiful day. It always seems to be on the last day. At 1:45 p.m. we would all meet at the pool to give Joe his present.

I was the first one back down to the pool. Kids began to arrive in dribbles. We all marched up to the lifeguard station and sang "For He's a Jolly Good Fellow." He was really surprised and thought we were going to throw him into the deep. I presented him with the disc saying, "Joe, you've been swimmingly super and this is a token of our appreciation." There was a sad good-bye, and we made our way to the waiting bus that took us to Wayne Newton's ranch for a barbeque.

What a spread this one was - Casa de Shenandoah. The place was surrounded by a white ranch-style fence. I don't know how many acres he had, but the ranch included ponds and brooks. As for livestock, he had sheepdogs, a few mongrels, swans, geese, ducks, peacocks, deer, kangaroos, 110 Arabian horses, and one beautiful little girl. His wife Elaine, who comes from Taiwan, is a doll. Both of them have pitch-black hair. Wayne put on a horse show for us. He had an employee at the ranch bring on the horses. We all sat on the ranch fence and grass fascinated as Alfredo walked these beautiful creatures through their paces.

My journal of our first Las Vegas gig ends here. Perhaps it was too sad to write anymore. Perhaps I was too tired to write another word.

The next day we flew back to New York, where the Nativity animals were waiting for us in the animal room. It may have been November 1st, but for us "it was beginning to look a lot like Christmas."

The swine flu was flying around the world. President Ford advised everyone to have a flu shot. Both Tom and I decided we wouldn't get it, but as soon as we walked past the animal room and saw the flies, we changed our minds. Flies were a big problem. We put fly paper up in the dressing room, but we had to be careful. The Toy Soldier hats were very tall, with a white feather plume sticking up about five inches above the hat. Sometimes the feather would get caught and stick to the fly paper.

During a break at our first Christmas rehearsal of the season, Tom and I went to Assembly, a restaurant on 51st Street between Fifth and Sixth Avenues, frequented by Music Hall personnel. Tom wanted to tell me about his train trip back across the country, and I was excited to tell him about going to Wayne Newton's ranch. He kept talking about a man he got to know on the train and how interesting he was. Tom kept saying Peter this and Peter that. I suggested that maybe we should invite Peter to dinner. Then I asked if Peter had a last name.

"Yes, Finch."

"Finch! Peter Finch? The Peter Finch? You rode the train across the country with Peter Finch?"

"Well, yeah, one of them," Tom casually replied. He went on to say that during the course of their conversation he'd mentioned that his wife was a Rockette. Peter Finch said, "Oh, I've done some things for Radio City." Fascinated, Tom asked, "Really, what did you do?"

"Oh, "Elephant Walk", "The Nun's Story" and "The Red Tent"."

Mr. Finch probably appreciated and liked Tom because Tom didn't know who he was, a famous actor, and simply appreciated him as an interesting and knowledgeable human being.

Looking back at my journal, I realize that I said all the stars that we saw were wonderful, terrific, beautiful, dolls, great, and one can wonder, was everyone that great? As my dad used to ask when Billy and I would go to the movies, "Did you kids ever see a bad movie? Are they all great?" Then we'd proceed to tell him about the coming attractions. "Gee, Dad, we've gotta see that one; it looks great." But when you've trained all your life, studying dance, voice and drama, and different kinds of dance, you're really appreciative of fellow artists. And sometimes critical, too. But playing Lake Tahoe and Las Vegas was such a great opportunity and eye opening experience for all of us. And the touring days had just begun. However, sinister days were on the horizon.

Easter of 1977 saw a Peter Gennaro produced, choreographed and directed show called "Top Hat and Tales," with a Top Hat salute to Fred Astaire featuring Susan Smith and Joe McGrath, and a "Mother Goose and Friends" ballet. "Hands and Hats" was the Rockette contribution, with choreography by Violet Holmes. The film accompanying the stage show was "Mr. Billion" starring Terence Hill, Valerie Perrine and Jackie Gleason.

One year later we would have a hapless Easter opening, and the preceding months would be full of sadness and worry. Even so, we all had a good laugh at dress rehearsal for the Easter show. It was again produced, choreographed and directed by Peter. Called "Springtime Carousel," it featured a delightful segment called "Bunny Follies." There were people dressed as bunnies dressed as people. A bunny trio dressed like the Andrews Sisters sang "A Tisket, A Tasket, I Found a Yellow Basket." And one very sultry bunny in a strapless gown sang "I've Got A Right to Sing the Blues." And then, we had a right to sing the blues too.

A press release from Patricia Robert was dated 1/5/78. "RADIO CITY MUSIC HALL TO CLOSE. The management of Radio City Music Hall announced today that the 6,000 seat theatre would be closed and the traditional format of a stage show and screen presentation terminated at the end of the 1978 Easter Show on April 12."

What had been predicted for years was finally becoming a very unpleasant and frightening reality. Many former employees had seen the glee club come and go, and many of us still kicking had seen the Ballet Company get their exit papers. I remembered the last night of the Ballet Company, when I went up to their dressing room and wished them all well and that I hoped they all got a Broadway show. It should be noted there that the ballet dancers in recent years were hired from show to show; they were no longer a resident company. On August 4, 1979, Variety had a headline for a column stating "MUSIC HALL TELLS UNIONS IT'S NOT PLAYING AROUND; MAKE A DEAL OR WE CLOSE." The foreboding headline of The Daily News that day (January 5, 1978) "RADIO CITY SHUTS IN APRIL".

The tale of doom had been looming with much more threatening implications in recent years. The Daily News dated Sunday, January 8, 1978 was "RADIO CITY EYED BY STOCK MART. Site could be new AMEX Hdq." Tom said of this, "As the Music Hall goes, so goes the Nation."

The Ballet, The Rockettes, various singers, musicians, stagehands, ushers, cashiers and other Music Hall employees formed the "Showpeople's Committee to Save Radio City Music Hall." On Thursday, January 19, 1978, we all received an URGENT mailing encouraging us to "encourage every concerned individual to write to their state senators and congressmen demanding they take immediate action in preventing the death of the Radio City

Music Hall format of stage show and movie." We were instructed to send our comments to editors of The New York Post, The New York Times, The Daily News, The Tribune and Our Town. The Showpeople's Committee had even secured an office for themselves in the Hilton Hotel on 53rd Street, between 6th and 7th Avenues. Letters were sent to the Mayor and a very eloquent letter to Cardinal Cooke stating that "For 45 years, literally in the shadow of St. Patrick's Cathedral, the seat of the Archdiocese of New York, Radio City Music Hall has brought entertainment, joy and culture to more than 250 million people from all over the world." It went on to state that when young people "were taken to the Music Hall by parents, they succumbed to the music of its Symphony Orchestra and went on to pursue the serious study of music . . ." Many performers who started at the Music Hall . . . i.e. Jan Pierce, Robert Merrill, Robert Weede and John Alexander, to name a few of the stars; Melissa Hayden, Nora Kaye and others in the field of Ballet." The pleas went on to ask His Eminence "to spread the word of our situation to the people of New York."

We had to work fast; and armed with petitions, we set out to get signatures. During a hiatus, Tom and I went across country by train, and I got signatures across the United States, including at Union Station in Chicago, where I got permission from the station master to parade around the station soliciting signatures. I would also get signatures on the bus ride going home, after the last show. Every New York bus driver granted me permission to get bus riders' signatures. Our petition read as follows:

"AS OF APRIL 12, 1978 RADIO CITY MUSIC HALL, SHOWPLACE OF THE NATION, IS DESTINED TO CLOSE ITS DOORS. WE, THE UNDERSIGNED, URGE THAT ALL NECESSARY ASSISTANCE BE GIVEN TO ENABLE RADIO CITY MUSIC HALL TO REMAIN OPEN IN ITS PRESENT STAGE SHOW, MOVIE FORMAT. THE MUSIC HALL, WITH ITS INTERNATIONALLY

FAMOUS STAGE SHOWS IS ONE OF NEW YORK'S MOST IMPORTANT TOURIST ATTRACTIONS AND SOURCE OF FAMILY ENTERTAINMENT. THE HALL ITSELF RANKS AMONG THE WORLDS MOST BEAUTIFUL ENTERTAINMENT FACILITIES AND IS AN INTEGRAL PART OF NEW YORK'S ARCHITECTURAL AND CULTURAL HERITAGE. THE MUSIC HALL'S CLOSING WOULD DEAL A SEVERE BLOW TO THE CITY'S ECONOMY AND THE HEARTS OF NEW YORKERS. PLEASE HELP US PREVENT THIS LOSS.

NAME STREET CITY STATE

There were press conferences and cocktail parties galore, with one very lavish party at Studio 54, where they celebrated Elizabeth Taylor's 46th birthday, and the pending exodus of the Rockettes. Everyone wanted to buy Elizabeth Taylor a drink and say good-bye to the Rockettes. It was like seeing who's going to come to your funeral. Studio 54 was packed, and we had an eyeful when upstage, floating in the air, was a quarter moon and a spoon that would dip sprinkles of imaginary cocaine. Another eyeful was the scantily clad waiters floating around in Roman togas.

It was a tearful time with a plethora of tears erupting down sixty cheeks (we had been reduced to thirty) as we did our final kicks on la passarelle (the runway), that followed the curve of the orchestra pit, thereby practically putting us on top of the front row. With each show, we got a standing ovation and along with a smile, the tears came down as we stood in the final cheesecake pose, enjoying our applause.

We were photographed on the steps of City Hall kicking up our heels with Lieutenant Governor Mary Ann Krupsak, a champion of our desire to save the Music Hall. The New York Post printed the picture in its Tuesday, March 14, 1978 edition. While posing on the City Hall steps, we were upstaged momentarily when photographers aimed their cameras skyward as the Concord flew overhead.

Prayer and perseverance paid off as the headline for the April 13th edition of the Daily News read: MUSIC HALL WINS REPRIEVE . . . STAYING OPEN FOR ANOTHER YEAR." We all breathed a sigh of relief.

A year later, we celebrated another magnificent headline, again in The Daily News on Friday, June 1, 1979: "RADIO CITY MUSIC HALL GALA OPENING."

The night before had been a segue into a new era for the Music Hall and the Rockettes. We had known a change was coming since the beginning of year. On February 27, 1979 we received a notice stating that the "Formation of a national entertainment production company, Radio City Music Hall Productions, Inc. was announced today by Alton G. Marshall, Chairman and President of Radio City Music Hall Corporation." There were conspiracy theories all over the place that this had been a set up all along. But, however it came about, the outcome was much to one's liking. The New York Post headline on April 13 was "2M DEAL SAVES MUSIC HALL."

We all received severance pay from one fading company, and eagerly began work for Radio City Music Hall Productions, Inc., a new enterprise and a subsidiary of Rockefeller Center, Inc. Former Vice-President and director of Walt Disney Productions Robert F. Jani would be President, Producer and CEO. The weekend section of the New York Times on Friday, June 1st stated "RADIO CITY MUSIC HALL RETURNS," with a cut line "The Rockettes restored to their original strength of 36 last night helped Radio City Music Hall begin a new era." It went on to say, "A New York Summer" unfolded. It's a show that does not know the word intimate, with larger than life sound and scenery."

Indeed. Pam, Carol and I sat out in the house one early rehearsal morning as Mr. Jani, way up in the back of the house, called off his direction to the stage manager on stage. "Now, the plane flies in. Then we bring on the ship, the train and the bus." Bob Jani had told us during a pep talk. "You'll probably never do anything like this again in your life." With nineteen numbers and one thousand costumes in the show, he was probably right. Bear in mind that the distance from the stage-right quick-change room to the stage-left quick-change room was a city block. Consequently, a costume might end up on stage left, but would have to be pre-set before the next show to make its entrance from the stage-right quick-change room.

Also displayed in this grandiose production was the Cherry Blossom Doncho Curtain, which is the largest silk curtain ever made in Japan, and was a gift to the people of New York from her sister city of Tokyo and the people of Japan. It had been presented to the City of New York on May 4, 1964.

A showman to the core, Bob Jani indulged in a very smart marketing ploy when he invited all the New York City hotel managers and their wives, and all the taxi drivers and their wives to a preview of "New York Summer." Excitement and nerves were pulsating as we prepared for our new opening.

With new (but a duplicate of the old) wallpaper and carpeting from the southern mills that had woven the original, and a brand new 90-minute dazzling stage show, we opened to the cheers of thousands, and a prestigious audience among them. Mayor Koch accompanied by Bess Meyerson, three mayoral predecessors, Abraham D. Beame, John V. Lindsay and Robert F. Wagner. Mrs. Nelson Rockefeller was there, as were Ginger Rogers, Harold Prince, Celeste Holm, Sylvia Miles, John Cameron Swayze, Barbara Walters, and Mr. & Mrs. Joseph F. Levine.

Radio City Music Hall had been the dream of another showman, Samuel L. Rothafel (Roxy) and when it first opened in December of 1932, with another illustrious list of stars including Clark Gable and Greer Garson, it had a much longer then 90-minute show. Some of the audience members back then probably thought they might be served breakfast, the show went on so long. But within a short period of time, they combined a film with a stage show, which turned out to be the winning formula for over 40 years.

Now, the Music Hall had come full circle and was back to a stage show only format, and the newly renamed Radio City Music Hall Entertainment Center, with its $5 million art deco restoration was beginning a new era–a spectacular era. Roberta Peters sang the Star Spangled Banner, and one of The New Yorkers singers jokingly said, as she walked up the aisle of the auditorium, "Play ball." We did play ball and the show and the new era began.

"A New York Summer" had a successful run during the summer of '79. Unlike the old regime, where we worked three or four weeks on seven days a week and then had a week off, which equated to a six day work week, now we had a real six day work week. Now the whole cast and crew worked six days a week, and Monday was our "dark" day. There were twelve 90-minute shows a week, with a matinee and evening performances.

"A New York Summer, a magical Musical Celebration" had its gala opening on May 31, 1979. Beginning with an organ prelude, this time using two console Wurlitzer organs, one on stage-right and on stage-left, the show was off to a glorious start. Mr. Jani spoke about all the preparations that had gone into renaming the Music Hall in the previous months. After Miss Peters sang the Star Spangled Banner, the overture began, conducted by Donald Pippin, and we were on our way. A spectacular tribute to the city of New York, the show began with The New Yorkers singing "New York, New York," followed by the entire company.

The Rockettes were dressed in white top hats and tails, plus white canes, and we ascended to stage level from the depth of the theatre, coming up on the #1 elevator. Tapping to "I Love New York." the applause came and was music to our ears. Strutting our stuff with the canes, we did a false exit, where dressers quickly tore off our long pants (stuck on by the magic of theatre - Velcro), and we made a re-entrance, now wearing the top hats, tails and nicely high-cut trunks.

The rest of the show was seen through the eyes of tourists, who took a taxi ride. There was a typical Manhattan street scene, a visit to the United Nations, where the Cherry Blossom Doncho Curtain was displayed, a fantasy visit to Central Park depicting both summertime and wintertime with ice statues, and a Harlem street scene with a group of boy dancers, The Apples, who did a terrific routine under a bridge. There was also a trip to Coney Island, a peak at New York nightlife, a salute to Broadway, a disco number dancing up a curl-a-cu (spiral) ramp, a shopping scene, and a visit to 100 year old St. Patrick's Cathedral; and finally, making our way to Rockefeller Center, and some Radio City Music Hall memories, and a grand finale.

Bob Jani had wanted to do a 50-year memory lane number of the Rockettes depicting the different routines we had performed throughout our 50 year history. The costume changes were so fast; we literally just had a chorus or less to change. What went on in the wings was hysterical–or what didn't get on the body. It had to be scrapped, but was later done in another production.

Besides our in-house costume designer, Frank Spencer, the Rockettes also had special costumes designed by Bob Mackie. Choreography and staging were by Violet Holmes, Dru Davis, Louis Johnson, Linda Lemac and Howard Parker. The whole production ran smoothly under the watchful eyes of Stage Manager Jeff Hamlin. There were five assistant stage managers: our own stage managers from the old days, George Cort and Frank Hawkins, plus assisting stage managers Peter Elencove, Linda Harris and Neil Jay Miller. With 68 people in the production staff, 93 people in the cast, and 42 in the orchestra, we all settled down for a nice long summer's run of "A New York Summer."

On our dark day, Monday, a lot of us would often go to Jones Beach or Robert Moses Beach. After a relaxing day on the sand, the evening would usually find us in Porky and Glen's, a terrific seaside restaurant run by an old sea salt. There's nothing like a dry martini and a steamed lobster after beaching all day.

We had an almost five month run with "A New York Summer" and then it was time to tour again. The New York State Department of Commerce sent us out on a mini-tour, a five day sweep across the United States. Our tour began on September 27, 1979 when United Air Lines flew us to San Francisco, where we performed in Union Square. We stayed at the St. Francis Hotel, and during some free time Carol, Pam, Eileen and I had a great boat trip down the San Rafael Canal, thanks to Eileen, who knew someone who had a boat. We had a great day boating under the Golden Gate Bridge. Before leaving San Francisco, we had a quick sightseeing tour of the Bay Area, with a stop at Jack London Square for shopping and a light lunch.

On the second leg of the tour, Braniff Air Lines took us to Dallas, where we stayed and performed at the Fairmont Hotel. I was flying alongside my roommate Joan Peer, when I happened to turn around to catch Eileen Collins pulling the arm rest out of her chair. She took one look at my face, which must have expressed that I thought the plane was falling apart, and burst out laughing. Eastern Air Lines took us on our last leg of the journey, to Miami Beach. We did a photo shoot in bikinis in the ocean, behind the Fontainebleau Hotel. We kicked and splashed in the most turquoise ocean water I've ever seen in my life.

Eastern flew us back to New York, but we weren't there long. With a couple of weeks of rehearsals behind us, on October 27th we had a 7:45 a.m. call to meet at the 51st Street stage door to board the bus to JFK Airport. United flight #777 was departing at 9:45 a.m. for Las Vegas, where we were to play the Hilton again–on the bill with Liberace. This time I had a warm bathrobe with me for that cold dressing room. The shining young star of Broadway's "Annie," Andrea McArdle, was on the bill with us. During this run, Andrea celebrated her sixteenth birthday and Liberace gave her an enormous ring. Andrea was a darling, unspoiled and talented young performer. The Rockettes adored her, and they adored Lee. He was wonderful to us.

Liberace invited us to his Las Vegas home, where he actually had two homes built together. In the living room there was a mirrored concert grand piano; in the guest room, a sable bedspread; on the dining room table, pearl place mats; and in Lee's bedroom, a ceiling adorned with angels in the Michelangelo style with Liberace as the center heavenly angel. Much to the dismay of the housekeepers, there were approximately seventeen dogs that inhabited this household. Siegfried and Roy were two of the many guests at this party.

We had been quite concerned as to how we were going to make this gig. The musicians back at the Music Hall had threatened to go on strike, at which time we had secured the Las Vegas engagement. In the end, the musicians did not go on strike and the Music Hall needed Rockettes at both the Music Hall and the Las Vegas Hilton. It took 76 girls to carry this thing off.

The Las Vegas engagement went without a hitch, except for one Saturday afternoon when I had walked to Skaggs Supermarket. I had figured I'd walk there and call my roommate, Joan Peer, to come pick me up in a taxi when I had all our groceries. After I finished shopping, I kept telephoning Joanie, but got no answer, again and again. Now, it was imperative that I get back in time in order to order room service (chicken and baked potato), prepare and eat a salad, and get done in time to go down to the dressing room in time for call. After repeated no-answers from Joan, I decided to call a taxi. If California had had a devastating earthquake and Las Vegas had become ocean-front property, Joanie would have slept through it. Finally, I just had to call a taxi. Fifteen minutes passed and no cab. Fifteen more minutes passed and still no cab. After 45 minutes of waiting, I called the taxi company and was told, "Lady, this is Saturday afternoon. You can't expect a cab that quickly." I waited fifteen more minutes and decided I could not wait any longer. Out of the parking lot I went with the supermarket cart and pushed the cart with the groceries up Joey W. Brown highway wondering all the way what the topography of the Hilton was like. Would I have to get this supermarket cart up stairs? I couldn't remember.

To my delight, when I reached the hotel there was a ramp, and I just wheeled the cart right up the ramp and across the casino. Not one person looked at me strangely; I felt as though I were at home in New York. Just an ordinary day's occurrence–a woman pushing a shopping cart with groceries and carrot tops peeking out of the bags as she wheeled her way across the casino to the elevator and pushed the cart into the elevator and pushed the button for the 27th floor. Joanie was shocked as I entered the room with the cart, and felt badly that she hadn't awakened when I'd phone her. At the same time, she laughed and was amazed to see a shopping cart full of groceries in our hotel room. I quickly called room service and ordered the baked chicken and potato, and prepared us a salad. We made call on time. Oh, and I brought the supermarket cart back the next day.

Since it was late in October, the days were a little cooler, so there weren't as much swimming pool shenanigans as on our previous visit. But there was shopping, and I bought three pairs of high heels that Carrie Bradshaw would have drooled over; they were made in Italy and gorgeous.

Liberace made his entrance being driven onstage by his chauffer in a magnificent Rolls Royce. I don't know which was more magnificent, his car or his wardrobe. One thing for sure, Lee was definitely magnificent–not only on stage, but in person, too. The ladies in the audience loved him and we did, too. When we got toward the end of the run, we started to think of getting Liberace a gift. But what does one give Liberace? A shirt? A tie? Nah. Then I had the idea to take a pair of our tap shoes and have them bronzed. "He can put them in his museum," I said. The plan was approved and I set out to find a shop that would do it. Well, when we presented the gift to Lee, gentleman that he was, he accepted them graciously, but he held them up in the air with a quizzical look on his face. The shoes came out terribly; I mean they were awful. I thought the Rockettes were going to lynch me. Fortunately, we had another gift for him, too.

During the last performance, Lee played the most beautiful Christmas medley for us, knowing that we were going back to Radio City to do the Christmas show. Some of us stood in the wings with tears in our eyes.

Back in New York by late November, we had immediate rehearsals, not only for the Christmas show, but also for the Macy's Thanksgiving Day Parade. We always had to go down to Macy's late the night before Thanksgiving to rehearse on the street in front of the store. Thirty-fourth Street was blocked off, so we could get our marks on the street. Dancing on the streets of New York was always a challenge. Not only could the weather be a challenge, but dancing on top of manhole covers or an irregular surface could be precarious.

We were supposed to go back to the Hall after our late night Macy's rehearsal for a Nativity rehearsal onstage, but we were too exhausted and went home and went to bed. The next day was Thanksgiving, which meant an early call to be bused to Macy's before the start of the parade and it was opening day at the Music Hall! As the old saying goes, when it rains, it pours. And it has rained on our parade.

One Macy's Thanksgiving we wore very elaborate zebra-striped hats, black and white striped with a hot-pink colored mane made of turkey feathers. Special plastic covers were made to protect the turkey feathers, but we were hoping not to have to wear them because the plastic cover mashed down the feathers. The weather was capricious. It would rain and then it would stop. It would rain again, and then it would stop. We put the plastic covers on and took them off, again and again. Finally, moments before we were to go on, we were instructed to take them off. Guess what? It rained! Not only did it rain, it was cold, so it was slushy. There's nothing like doing a routine in white tights on a cold, slushy day in front of Macy's on national television.

Thanksgiving of '79 we were so numb from jet lag and all the rehearsals for Macy's and the Christmas show, it probably wouldn't have mattered what the weather was like. We were so rehearsed and so tired that we went across 51st Street to Schrafft's on a very, very short break. The waiter felt so badly for us, I actually got a martini to go in a Styrofoam cup.

It was good to be back home, but before we knew it, the Christmas season was over and it was January 7, 1980, and we were again meeting at the 51st St. stage door for a return engagement with Liberace at the Las Vegas Hilton.

This time my roommate was Susan Theobald. Susie and her sister had been ballet girls, but when the Ballet Company was cut, Susie went out and learned to tap. I always thought Susan deserved a tremendous amount of credit for that. It's not an easy thing to do when on has been trained in ballet all one's life, but she did it.

At the end of January, we flew back to New York, but not for long. This time, the New York State Department of Commerce was sending us to London. We were going to play the prestigious Royal Albert Hall. On the two previous Las Vegas visits, Tom had to stay in New York because he was needed at Radio City; but we were on hiatus during the London tour and he was able to come with us.

On the evening of February 4, 1980, we boarded British Airways flight 174 for London. Within 15 minutes of our 8:00 p.m. departure from JFK we were flying over Nantucket. I loved our British pilot, whoever he was. He talked to us often in the most charming accent, and his flight was smooth. Descending through the early morning white clouds over England was like going into a fairytale. Hail Britannia. Then I thought I knew how Mary Poppins must feel every time she descends over London. Well, that may be a bit of a stretch, since she used an umbrella and we were in a 747, but it was very fantasy-like. When we disembarked, I just looked at that 747 in awe. How on earth do they ever get that thing in the air, much less across the ocean?

After everyone went through customs and had reclaimed their luggage, we were bused to the London Hilton. We were bused on the "wrong" side of the street. Oh, that was disarming! Finally, we reached the Hilton, where we were going to perform. We checked in, exhausted after the all-night flight, but with the 5-hour time difference, it was now Greenwich Time and time for a London breakfast. Tom and I ordered room service and then tried to take a nap, which was difficult since we were so excited to be in Europe for the first time in our lives. Between jet lag and the excitement of being in England, sleep was difficult to come by and a walk on the British streets was luring us to go see the sights.

Amazingly, we were free for the day, and since we had only five days in London, it seemed more imperative to take advantage of the free time, rather than sleep. Any tourist would know what I'm talking about. Actually, we were free a good deal of the time., with the exception of possible press interviews. In fact, there was an evening press reception that first night at the Roof Top Restaurant at the Hilton. It was an hour and a half press conference, and we were all required to be there.

But the next morning, on opening day of Royal Albert Hall, we had a 7:30 a.m. call to board the bus that would take us to Royal Albert Hall for rehearsal. It was a matinee only for our premiere performance at RAH, so a tight timetable was in place for musicians, singers, Rockettes, and the rest of our company to rehearse. This also included the gathering of our costumes for a cast of 40, as all of the wardrobe had been shipped to London a few days ahead of us. The "I Love New York" rehearsal began at 8:00 a.m. and concluded at 10:00 a.m. Costume unpacking and arranging began at 8:00 a.m. and was scheduled to go to 11:30 a.m. So there we were, on the other side of "the pond" putting on makeup and checking to see if our costumes were pre-set in the appropriate place.

At noon, Greenwich time, our gala performance began on London's prestigious Royal Albert Hall. The following is what Trevor Fishlock of the London Times of February 2, 1980 wrote of our performance; the text appeared under a photo of the Rockettes' lineup at RAH.

"Well-tuned machine: Anachronistic in their wholesomeness, the Rockettes of Radio City, New York, danced their energetic way into the affections of Londoners yesterday. They are cheerful, long-legged ladies who earn their living by dressing in exiguous iridescent costumes, shiny tights and silvery shoes (as well as jaunty feathers in their caps) and who wheel their way around the stage of the Radio City Music Hall in New York, kicking up their legs in unison. They have been doing this for half a century and have become an American institution. Connoisseurs of the high-kicking art regard them as entirely non-erotic: The Rockettes are seen as a well-tuned machine, a relic of an age of stricter mores. Yesterday they were giving their high-stepping all at the

Albert Hall with the aim of persuading more Britons to visit New York."

Wow! How's that for a cutline? There'll always be an England. Such vocabulary! How about that word Exiguous? I don't know if the Rockettes cared much for the word "non-erotic." Than again, Peter Allen referred to us in his show as "36 little June Allysons getting off the bus . . . with their tap shoes on."

The Rockettes and the New Yorkers were not the only Americans performing at the Royal Albert Hall. There were also some stars from the Metropolitan Opera and guest appearances made by Carol Channing and Yul Brynner. Since this whole production was a joint venture between British Airways and the New York State Department of Commerce, the mission was to promote tourism and to sell Britishers on the joys, fun, glamour and Yankee culture of "The Big Apple."

Again we tried to tap dance our way into Londoners' hearts with our final night in London with the evening performance of our "I Love New York" show in the Coronation Room at the London Hilton. This 5-day London gig was the first time the Rockettes had been abroad since winning the Grand Prix at the Paris Exposition in 1937.

We had so much free time during this 5-day period that we all managed to squeeze in a bit of London sightseeing, which was thrilling to behold. Since Tom was such a train buff, he rode the Tube (London's subway) again and again. Well, I liked the Tube, too, but not all day. I heard that Dottie Belle Meymann had booked herself on a sightseeing bus touring the countryside outside London, so I quickly made arrangements to join her. The only two Americans on the bus, Dot and I had a very enjoyable tour taking in Oxford College and then going into the beautiful English countryside with a visit to Stratford-upon-Avon, and seeing William Shakespeare's and Anne Hathaway's thatched roof cottage.

One free evening, our whole company went to Beefeater by the Tower of London, complete with medieval-style eating with the fingers and jostling; we all had a smashingly bloody good time. In fact, Carol Toman gave one of the horseback riders her scarf for good luck. She was shocked when he said to her, "You, of course, know what this means." I got a kick out of being near where Anne Boleyn got the axe, since my mother had told me she named me after Anne Boleyn with the cautionary words, "Never lose you head over a man."

Many of our company headed back to New York after our 5-day stay in London, but some of us stayed behind a bit longer. Since we were still on hiatus from the Music Hall, Tom booked a 10-day tour of the Continent for us. We took the Boat-Train from Folkstone to Calais, where Tom exchanged a necktie clip with the conductor on the train. Train buffs are the same all over the world. From Folkstone, we boarded the boat and sailed past the White Cliffs of Dover while crossing the English Channel. From Calais, we boarded the French National Railroad and with our Eurailpass, Nous avons arrivé au Paris. Since the London Hilton had been so good to us, Tom decided to continue staying at a Hilton; so we found ourselves on the Left Bank at the Paris Hilton. We could see the Eiffel Tower from our window.

Ever the transit buff, Tom had us walking to the Paris Metro from our hotel on our first morning in Paris. We happened to walk past a hostling area and I was so proud of myself when a very pretty German girl approached us and asked us in French for the directions to the hosteling area. I was able to tell her in French, since we had just walked by a slew of bicycles. As soon as she heard my French, she started to speak in English. Oh, c'est dommage!

Actually, the same sort of thing happened in London right in front of Buckingham Palace. I was preparing to cross the street, looking up and down for oncoming traffic, when a chap stopped me and said, "You're an American, aren't you?" When I nodded in the affirmative he added, "You be careful now." It dawned on me later that I wasn't looking towards oncoming traffic the way one would look in London. I was looking the way we would look in the States.

Not only do I have to say I love Paris in the springtime, but in the wintertime, summertime, any other time. What a beautiful city. We couldn't believe we were walking along the Champs-Élysée, stopping at Maxim's for lunch, seeing the Arc de Triomphe, la Seine, and Notre Dame Cathedral. The only c'est dommage part was that we had only three days in Paris.

Prior to this déjeuner in Paris, back in New York, between shows, Tom and I had dinner in a Chinese restaurant. I was talking excitedly about this pending European trip and asked Tom whether, if I could arrange it, would he like to come to Europe with us? He immediately started singing, "I'll Take You to Maxine's." So walking in Paris, we happened to pass by Maxine's; Tom tried to shy away from it until I started singing "I'll Take You to Maxine's." Our charming French waiter said to us, "Ze martinis are your poison; ze wine is ours."

From Paris we trained on to Wuppertal, West Germany, home of the only suspended monorail in the world: die Schwebebahn. This was the thrill of a lifetime for Tom, who had read, studied and digested all the facts of this monorail. In fact, Tom was at one time vice-president of a San Francisco-based monorail company. This company was trying to sell the Bay Area on the merits of having a suspended monorail, even one that went across the Oakland-Bay Bridge. While working for that company, Tom came back east to wait for orders to go to South America to help build a monorail. Since he had a background in theatre, he worked a couple of Broadway shows and went into Radio City to fill in temporarily. In the meantime, there was a revolution in South America, which ended all plans for the monorail project, and Tom ended up spending twenty-four years at Radio City. Incidentally, Wuppertal is also the home of Bayer Aspirin. Mr. Bayer invented his aspirin there.

When that German monorail pulled into its stop, driven by a lady driver, the look and excitement on Tom's face was like that of a little boy seeing his first train. We took the monorail on all eight miles of its trip, from Vohwinkel to Oberbarmen. We got off the monorail at Oberbarmen and walked around the town. Later, we stopped at a food stand and had a hot dog and Coke. When the young German clerk found out we were tourists from America, he said, "On zee house."

Back at the Kaiserhof Hotel that evening, we picked up a pitcher of ice from the desk clerk, since Europeans are not prone to putting ice into their cocktails the way Americans are. The desk clerk cautioned Tom, who was wearing a necktie with railroad symbols on it, to be careful of his necktie. "Oh, what's that about?" I asked. "Earlier that day we were out in a little shopping area and I was posing for a picture that Tom was taking as I stood by the statue of a woman with the Dutch-style wooden shoes on her feet. As I was posing with my foot in a position like the statue's, I saw a man walking towards me. From the other direction came two young girls who proceeded to walk up to the man and cut off his necktie."

The desk clerk explained that it was "Old Woman Carnival." It had to do with women's lib and that on this particular day (February 14, Valentine's Day), any German man, or for that matter any man wearing a necktie, was in danger of having his tie cut off. I'm sure there's some symbolism there somewhere.

We went out to an interesting dinner, interesting because we went to an Italian restaurant where we spoke neither Italian nor German, and the staff there spoke little or no English.

When we went back to the hotel to return the ice pitcher to the clerk, we stepped inside the inner lobby area where a television was broadcasting news of the Winter Olympics from Lake Placid, New York. Why we went in to hear this commentary is a little nebulous, since the report on the games was in German. Out of nowhere darted two frauleins who headed straight for Tom and cut off his train-symboled necktie. As Tom tried to protest, the desk clerk and I were hysterical with laughter.

More than twenty years have passed since then, and I wonder if women's liberation has gained any advancement in Germany, so that men no longer have to tolerate having their neckties cut off on Valentines Day.

Our last stop on our "if it's Tuesday, it must be Belgium" trip was Rome. We were back at the Hilton, this time the Cavaleri Hilton, right near the Vatican. When we got off Eurail's "Palatino Express" in Rome, it was your typical, extremely busy railroad station. We engaged a young man named Giovanni in conversation. He had just come back from Vermont, where he had been studying police work. Giovanni was so kind to us, giving us not only instructions on how to get to our hotel, but also some Italian coins, since we had to have exact change to board a bus.

We were in a tremendous square with a crossroads of streets, and we had to find the exact spot of the bus stop. We passed some policia who were holding rifles, which made me nervous; I wasn't used to seeing police holding rifles. (This was long before 9/11). I asked in my limited Italian, "Scusa, l'autobus, l'autobus, nove nove nove?" (Giovanni had told us to take # 999).

"Ecola," they responded, pointing to the bus stop. I was so proud of myself again having gotten us on the right bus in a strange country, but we didn't know where to get off the bus. So there we were riding, riding, riding through the seven hills of Rome. People got on the bus; people got off the bus. We were sitting right behind the bus driver, a very handsome man who looked like Rosano Brazzi. When he was obviously at the end of his route, he turned to us as if to say, "Why did you not get off anywhere? I am at the end of my run." We showed him our picture of the Cavaleri Hilton and he directed us as best he could in language barrier directions to our hotel. So, we started walking up one of the seven hills of Rome and finally made it to our hotel.

Since we'd heard about very expensive taxi rides in Rome, and since Tom had his love affair with trains and mass transit, we took the subway (the Metropolitan) through Rome with its very Latin, ancient Roman named subway stops like Octavia, Calpurnia, Augusta and Caesar. Tom had taken a very small tape recorder of mine with him and it was really quite a sight to see him holding the microphone to record the screeching sounds of the Italian subway as we screeched around a curve, and all these Italians looking on in disbelief as this train buff recorded the train sounds (music only to a train buff's ears).

We both got a kick out of the number of cats running around the Coliseum, as if they were representing their much larger ancestors who were part of the history of the Coliseum when Christians were fed to the lions.

After our Roman holiday we headed back to London for our return flight across the Atlantic. This time we were in a Boeing 707 and on a lot bumpier ride than our smooth 747 flight. We arrived back in New York on February 20th, and on the 22nd immediately began rehearsals for the March 14th opening of the Easter Show. Though I didn't know it at the time, this was to be my last Easter Show at Radio City.

Opening on March 14, 1980, "It's Spring - the Holiday Spectacular" featured the Vienna Boys Choir, The Famous People Players, The New Yorkers (singers & dancers), illusionist Dan Witkowski, and the Rockettes with all of us accompanied by the Radio City Music Hall Orchestra. Not only did this Easter production feature Anton Rubinstein's "Kamenoi Ostrow," but also Franz Schubert's "The Twenty Third Psalm" and Jacob Gallus' "Hau Dies." Of course, our little master singers, the Vienna Boys Choir, were featured singers in this segment. This is where I went into my Florence Nightingale mode and rescued that fainting little Vienna choir boy. The boys also did a medley of songs from their featured part in the show. "On Spring Holiday From Vienna."

These adorable boys could be seen walking the New York City streets in unison between shows, wearing their uniformed navy blue coats. Everyone would stop and stare at them, they were so cute. One night after the show, Tom and I ran into them in a McDonalds as they were all having after the last show snacks. Downing a milk shake, one of them said, "Very cold shake."

This Easter show, conceived and produced by Robert F. Jani, with the Rockettes choreography by Violet Holmes, also featured The Famous People Players, a Canadian black light theatre group, which was founded in 1974 by Diane Duprey, who was also the artistic director of this amazing company. Ten of the company of thirteen were mentally challenged. However, in spite of their disability, they presented a fascinating combination of theatrical magic and puppetry.

During the run of this show we also taped a TV show up at Lincoln Center that starred Hal Linden. Mr. Linden was wonderful to work with and at the conclusion of the taping he presented all of us with a lithograph of an apple he had commissioned himself, since the show we did with him was all about "The Big Apple."

One May 2nd we opened a new show called "A Rockette Spectacular." which starred a wonderful dancing Hollywood legend, Miss Ginger Rogers. I don't think it's a stretch to say we were all in awe of the beautiful blond who danced with Fred . . . you know who. After seeing so many Fred Astaire and Ginger Rogers movies as a kid, I couldn't believe we were dancing on the same stage with this breathtaking screen legend.

Donald Pippin was executive musical director and he had one of the music greats, Sammy Cahn, work with him on special material. Together they created music and lyrics to "Alike, Alike," a number done by the Rockettes, "My Big Moment," Miss Rogers's solo, and "You're At the Music Hall" for the entire cast finale.

Following the overture, the Rockettes marched into the commencement of the show with "The West Point March." After the Rockettes' exit, the spotlight shines on the star's dressing room. Miss Rogers and her maid, played by Gail Nelson, talk show-biz. The maid asked Miss Rogers if she was nervous to appear in front of 6,000 people. It then segues into a rehearsal dance sequence with Ginger Rogers dancing with a dozen male dancers. She then did a medley of songs she had sung and danced to with the incomparable Fred. Ginger then introduced the Rockettes, where we did a medley of our own, a medley of dance routines done over the years. This was a series of routines Bob Jani had wanted to do for a long time, honoring the 50 year history of the Rockettes.

Before the "You're At The Music Hall" finale with the entire cast, the Rockettes did another great cowgirl number. This one was choreographed by Violet Holmes and Joyce Dwyer. This cowgirl number was quite different from Russell and Emily's cowboy routine. For one thing, we wore entirely different costumes–more cowgirlish. We wore hot pink blouses with rhinestone studded white vests, short skirts, a white hat with rhinestones around the brim, gators that looked like boots slipped over our silver tap shoes, and to top it off, a silver neckerchief. I guess you could say we were rhinestone cowgirls.

The run of the show was extended, but they forgot to tell the star about it and she had other commitments, so on June 2nd Carol Lawrence replaced Ginger Rogers. Miss Lawrence had just one short rehearsal with the entire cast, but she stepped into the spotlight beautifully. When I went down on stage, I witnessed Tom approach a pensive-looking Carol Lawrence and ask her if she would like a room in which to vocalize. Now you know, when you ask a singer something like that, you have a friend for life. She was most appreciative and later told me, "You have a wonderful husband."

The "Rockette Show's" final performance was on June 22nd and I had written in my journal that day, "What are we getting into next?" Just like in the old days, during the run of this show, we began rehearsals for another show. Before the June 27th opening of "Manhattan Showboat" however, we had a day off amidst a very heavy rehearsal schedule, and Carol Toman, her boyfriend Ramon Paracat, Phyllis Wujko, Holly Hunter and I all headed for Robert Moses beach. Later on we met up with Pam Kelleher, her boyfriend Dr. Jerry Halpern and Tom.

The next day one rehearsal schedule looked like this:

11:00 a.m.–2 p.m.	Orchestra Recording Studio
3:00 p.m.–6 p.m.	Orchestra Recording Studio
12 p.m.–5 p.m.	Cast (including Rockettes) Large Rehearsal Hall Piece together the show.
7:00 p.m.–10 p.m.	Large Rehearsal Hall Run through transitions

We had 5 fittings sandwiched in between rehearsing.

On June 25th my planner read as follows:

11:00 a.m.–2 p.m.	Orchestra Studio - Reading
12:00 noon–5 p.m.	Full Cast - Large Hall Run throughs & work sessions as needed
7 p.m.–12 midnight	Full Cast - Stage Crew - Tech work-through with Click Tracks

Actually went through show twice today. We were excused at 9:55 p.m. Never got onstage; they weren't ready. You should see all the stuff on stage - unbelievable! Saw Daisy, the elephant, today.

The following day was pretty much the same schedule, only this day we worked from noon to midnight. The official opening of the show was June 30th. After the second show that night, a cast party was held for us at Manhattan Plaza on 43rd Street, where they just happened to have a swimming pool. Boy did that swim feel good after all these rehearsals and opening day.

Karen Anders played Captain Belle, the skipper of "Manhattan Showboat," which took a sail down memory lane, sailing to the Copacabana, the Rainbow Room, a stop at the port of big bands with the likes of Benny Goodman and Duke Ellington. Cruising further back in time, there was a sail to Vaudeville to visit the Dolly Sisters, Eva Tanguay, Will Rogers, Jimmy Durante, Baby Snooks and W.C. Fields. There was even a port-of-call to P.T. Barnum and the circus.

Violet choreographed a terrific routine for us called "Vamps." We wore all black: black satin blouses, black satin loose-fitting slacks, very chic tight fitting hats and white tap shoes. With different musical rhythms, we segued in and out of all kinds of Vamps.

A memo from Patricia Robert dated July 15, 1980, stated: "PLEASE POST IMMEDIATELY - Fred Conrad, New York Times Photographer will be at the 2:30 p.m. performance of Manhattan Showboat tomorrow, July 16. Please alert Neil Miller and Thomas St. John to be on deck at 1:45 p.m. backstage. Keith Sherman will meet Mr. Conrad at the Executive Door at 1:45 p.m. and take him backstage to photograph Mr. Miller and Mr. St. John."

In an article by Richard F. Shephard, the July 25th 1980 edition of the New York Times wrote: "In 'Manhattan Showboat' a 90 minute tribute to New York theatre and music of the times, a large orchestra is raised 12 ½ feet above stage level, then is lowered and moved forward and dropped into a pit. A five-ton boat emerges through swirling mist and its hull splits in two to disgorge more entertainment. A circus, with an elephant and a cannon that shoots a dummy across the stage, fills tone scene." Mr. Shephard also wrote that Mr. Miller cued Mr. St. John, "Steam curtain, go." Mr. St. John grasped a lever unloosing the fog and, as the dense clouds dissipated to a great roar and rumble of sound, the showboat's prow came into view. The boat is the largest scenic element designed for the Music Hall, and it is illuminated by 2,000 lights."

In this show, the cast of 88 dressed and undressed out of 700 costumes, twice a day. Remember what I said at the beginning of this book about all that dressing and undressing?

The Republican National Convention had occurred in July and that great boy actor and former president of the Screen Actors Guild, and later on known as the Great Communicator, Ronald Reagan was the Presidential nominee.

In August, we entertained the delegates from the Democratic Party and someone very wisely and politically correctly commandeered one of the Nativity donkeys into action to accompany Daisy, the elephant from the finale of "Manhattan Showboat." Prior to show time, we posed for pictures with some of the delegates, and then went out on stage working our fannies off. Who gets a standing ovation? Piedro, the donkey! When he walked onstage, Piedro was wearing a red, white and blue straw hat. He was a Yankee Doodle Donkey!

The Music Hall had ordered 6,000 turkey dinners for the delegates. When the dinners arrived, they had all gone bad, so RCMH had to scrounge around to get 6,000 box lunches. Everyone from the Rainbow Room to Kentucky Fried Chicken had to prepare lunches for the delegates. We waved good-bye to the Democratic delegates and would soon be saying good-bye to "Manhattan Showboat." The show was originally slated to go into November, but on September 24th there was a notice on the call board that, due to the Grateful Dead Rock Concert coming in earlier, we would close "Manhattan Showboat" on October 15th. Nevertheless, it had a respectful run.

So, we had a short hiatus, but with a nip in the air it was beginning to feel a lot like Christmas again, and we already had one of the donkeys in the house. After a couple of weeks of prep rehearsals, we opened the Christmas Show on November 21st, a late opening for a Christmas Show. The "Magnificent Christmas Spectacular" was a repeat of last year's Christmas show and because of tradition and expense it would be repeated for five years.

Before show time there was a Christmas caroling in the Grand Foyer by The New Yorkers, dressed in Dickensian costumes. "Deck The Halls" began the overture, followed by the Christmas Tree "O Tannenbaum." Scene two featured a child ballerina dancing highlights from Tchaikovsky's "The Nutcracker Suite." Petite Amy Dolan danced splendidly with bicycle-riding panda bears, Russian teddy bears, a pas de quatre with some hippopotami, the Nutcracker and, of course, the handsome prince. In the third scene there was a little of "A Christmas Carol," Charles Dickens' famous story of the ages. Following were The Traditions of Santa Claus, The Night Before Christmas, International Holiday Traditions, The Hanukkah Festival, The Twelve Days of Christmas, The New Yorkers singing "Sing A Little Song" and concluding with the Rockettes and their "Parade of the Wooden Soldiers."

With Sammy Davis, Jr. at the party he gave for our cast in his star suite at Harrah's Lake Tahoe. This was our first time away from home (RCMH) since The Rockettes played The Paris Exposition in 1937.

At Liberace's home in Las Vegas. We were on the bill with him at The Las Vegas Hilton. Lee was a wonderful host, and, of course, the audiences loved him as did we.

Tom at the control board. When Frank Sinatra saw Tom at this submarine looking panel, he shouted to Tom "Dive! Dive! Dive!"

(l-r) Pam, me, and Carol in the "I Go To Rio" costumes from The Peter Allen Show.

1981

The Rockette Show starring Ginger Rogers. This show had its run extended, but they forgot to tell the star, who had other commitments. Carol Lawrence stepped in for Miss Rogers.

1980

all photos from the author's personal collection

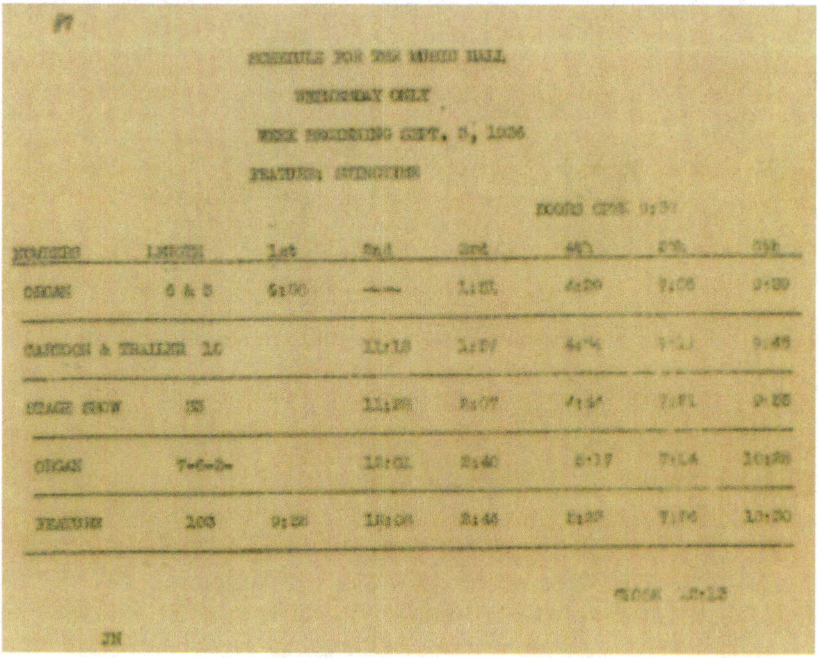

SCHEDULE FOR THE MUSIC HALL

WEDNESDAY ONLY

WEEK BEGINNING SEPT. 5, 1936

FEATURE: SWINGTIME

DOORS OPEN [illegible]

NUMBERS	LENGTH	1st	2nd	3rd	4th	5th	6th
ORGAN	6 & 5	9:00	——	1:21	4:20	7:05	9:20
CARTOON & TRAILER	10		11:18	1:57	[illegible]	[illegible]	9:45
STAGE SHOW	35		11:28	2:07	[illegible]	[illegible]	9:55
ORGAN	7-6-2-		12:03	2:40	5:17	7:54	10:28
FEATURE	103	9:28	12:08	2:46	[illegible]	[illegible]	10:30

CLOSE [illegible]

JN

RADIO CITY
MUSIC HALL
SHOW PLACE OF THE NATION
ROCKEFELLER CENTER

RADIO CITY MUSIC HALL

W. G. VAN SCHMUS, Managing Director

WEEK BEGINNING THURSDAY, FEBRUARY 11, 1937

PROGRAM

1. MUSIC HALL GRAND ORGAN

Richard Leibert at the Console

2. "THE MARCH OF TIME"

Produced by the Editors of "Time"
Released by RKO-Radio—February Issue

The Music Hall Stage Shows are produced under the Direction of
LEON LEONIDOFF, Senior Producer
RUSSELL MARKERT, Associate Producer

3. "VARIATIONS"
A Music Hall Revue

Produced by Leon Leonidoff
Settings by Bruno Maine
Costumes designed by M. Montedoro
—Executed by H. Rogge

A. "B Flat Minor Concerto"—Tschaikowsky
First Movement
Played for the first time by twelve pianists.
Featuring—Henrietta Schumann and Julia Glass

Dorothy Pearcy	Jane Courtland
Alberta Masiello	Clara Dayton
Diane Bernhard	Louise Sorensen
Vivian Rivkin	Mary Allison
Mildred Victor	Lillian Estrin

Music Hall Symphony Orchestra
Erno Rapee, Conductor
Mischa Violin, Jules Silver,
Associate Conductors

AFTER THE SHOW
Take Crosstown Bus (3 Blocks) to

Casino Entrance
50th Street and
Lexington Avenue
Bus Stops at Entrance

Dinner from $1.50
Supper Specialties from 75 cents

Cocktail Hour in Keyhole Bar-Lounge
MUSIC BY CORAL ISLANDERS

CASINO MONTCLAIR
HOTEL MONTCLAIR
LEXINGTON AVENUE AT 49TH STREET
OPEN EVERY DAY INCLUDING SUNDAYS

Hal Hope and His Swing-Rhythm Orchestra Play From 7 P.M. to Closing

(Program Continued)

B. "Happy Feet"
Music Hall Rockettes
(Dances by Gene Snyder)

C. "Buster Shaver, With Olive and George"

D. "Cavalcade of Irving Berlin's Famous Songs"
Jan Peerce
Music Hall Glee Club
(Vin Lindhe, Director)

E. "Midnight Blue"
Choreography by Florence Rogge
Hilda Eckler
Music Hall Corps de Ballet
(Florence Rogge, Director)
Entire Company

4. "ON THE AVENUE"

MUSIC AND LYRICS BY IRVING BERLIN
PRODUCED BY DARRYL F. ZANUCK
DIRECTED BY ROY DEL RUTH
A 20TH CENTURY-FOX PICTURE

CAST

Gary Blake	DICK POWELL
Mimi Caraway	MADELEINE CARROLL
Mona Merrick	ALICE FAYE
Ritz Brothers	THEMSELVES
Commodore Caraway	GEORGE BARBIER
Frederick Sims	ALAN MOWBRAY
Aunt Fritz	CORA WITHERSPOON
Jake Dibble	WALTER CATLETT
Eddie Eads	DOUGLAS FOWLEY
Herman	STEPIN FETCHIT
Miss Katz	JOAN DAVIS
Joe Cherry	PAUL GERRITS
Herr Hanfstangel	SIG RUMANN
Joe Papaloupas	BILLY GILBERT
Mr. Trivet	DOUGLAS WOOD
Harry Morris	PAUL IRVING
Luigi	RICARDO MANDIA
Stage Manager	JOHN SHEEHAN
Cabby	E. E. CLIVE
Kelly	HARRY STUBBS
Potts	EDWARD COOPER

MADELEINE CARROLL
ALICE FAYE
DICK POWELL

Contour curtain made under the Ted Weidhaas patents by Peter Clark, Inc. · Scenery built by Nolan Brothers and painted by Van Ackerman. · Shoes by I. Miller. · Ballet shoes by La Mendola. · The Program Cover designed by Benrimo employs, as the motif, one of the medallions by Hildreth Meiere on the outside south wall of the Music Hall. Steinway Pianos are used at The Music Hall. · This program subject to change without notice. Fabrics for costumes and scenery by Gladstone Silks.

Let's save the Music Hall for all of us

'When people care they do something about it.'

By PENNY SINGLETON

RADIO CITY MUSIC HALL is the showplace of the nation. There is no other establishment in our country to equal Radio City Music Hall. It is unique in its operation and is today the only example left of show business as it was.

Show business is a luxury business and whenever there is a national economic crunch, show business and show people are among the first to feel the impact of such crises. That is precisely what is happening today at the Music Hall. Attendance and the box office at the Music Hall had been decreasing steadily over the past years.

When bargaining between unions and management begins, it is normal for rumors to be circulated. Such rumors are sometimes identified as either management or union propaganda. Call it what you will, today's rumor can well be a reality. With all indications that it is possible, the Music Hall may have to close.

The American Guild of Variety Artists is the first union up to bat when negotiations begin at the Hall and New Yorkers may not know it was the union, AGVA, the Rockettes and all the performers at the Music Hall who three years ago gave up 14 weeks of employment and income in order to keep the Music Hall open. The performers were the first to contribute to keeping the Music Hall open by accepting the 14 week lay-off period. That was three years ago. Believe me, cutting down 52 weeks of employment to 38 weeks was a big sacrifice on the part of the Rockettes and all the performers at the Music Hall, and their union.

At the present time there are three negotiations on the table at the Music Hall: 1) AGVA, the union representing the world famous and talented Rockettes, the outstanding choral artists, and the world renowned Music Hall ballet and the spectacular acts from all over the world you see on stage at the Music Hall. 2) IATSE, the stage hands union, now sitting at the bargaining table. 3) The American Federation of Musicians, the union representing the world famous Music Hall orchestra. The AFM negotiation follows the stage hands bargaining.

When people care, they do something about it. The Rockettes, the union and all the performers at the Music Hall cared enough to contribute to keeping the Hall open three years ago. Will New Yorkers now step forward and see to it by public demand that the Music Hall is made a landmark? Will New Yorkers, who have the pride we have in the Music Hall begin the process of putting into action the steps necessary to save the Music Hall and the Rockettes and all the talented artists and shows from slipping into oblivion? We contributed thre years ago and it's your turn now, Mr. & Mrs. New York, to help us save Radio City Music Hall, the Rockettes, and those unforgettable Easter and Christmas shows on stage at Radio City Music Hall.

(Penny Singleton is the Executive President of the American Guild of Variety Artists.)

RADIO CITY MUSIC HALL CORPORATION
ROCKEFELLER CENTER
NEW YORK, N. Y. 10020

OFFICE OF
EXECUTIVE VICE PRESIDENT

August 10, 1976

Miss Penny Singleton
American Guild of Variety Artists
1540 Broadway
New York, New York 10036

Dear Miss Singleton:

As you know, we are currently engaged in negotiations with A.G.V.A., as well as several other unions. Should we reach a satisfactory agreement with all the unions concerned by September 1, 1976, then pursuant to Article 14 of our collective bargaining agreement, this letter will advise you that we will invoke the provisions of said Article in the manner described herein.

As required by Article 14.3, Radio City Music Hall hereby advises you that a "seasonal layoff" period shall occur effective September 9, 1976 through November 3, 1976. Our traditional policy will be reinstituted on November 4, 1976. Recalls for rehearsals shall commence on Monday, November 1, 1976.

Of course, in the event that we do not reach an agreement with all the unions, this notice will be academic, in that the theatre will close permanently on September 8, 1976.

If you have any questions, please contact me.

Sincerely,

Charles R. Hacker

CHARLES R. HACKER
Executive Vice President

CRH:ah

Happy Birthday
Mr. President

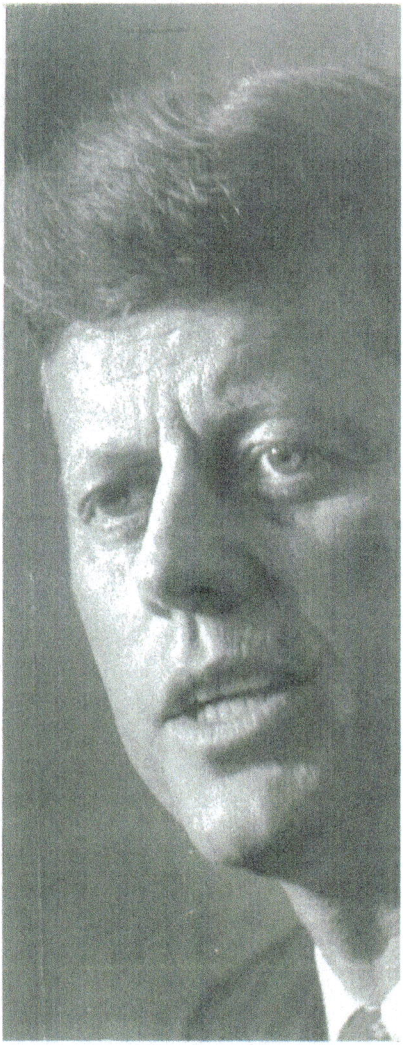

JAMES A. FARLEY
MRS. FRANKLIN D. ROOSEVELT
HERBERT H. LEHMAN
ROBERT F. WAGNER
Honorary Chairmen

ANNA M. ROSENBERG
ARTHUR B. KRIM
Chairmen

FRANCIS J. QUILLINAN
Treasurer
THOMAS J. ROURKE
Comptroller

ROBERT W. DOWLING
Chairman Finance Committee

MRS. THOMAS R. HESS
JOHN I. SNYDER
KENNETH P. STEINREICH
Co-Chairmen Finance Committee

ROBERT S. BENJAMIN
DOROTHY HIRSHON
FREDERICK W. RICHMOND
Associate Chairmen

HARRIS J. KLEIN
Coordinator

GEORGE BACKER
HARRY BRANDT
SAMUEL BRISKMAN
DANIEL BURROWS
O. ROY CHALK
RAYMOND C. DEERING
IRVING M. ENGEL
MRS. MARSHALL FIELD
JAMES L. GARRITY
MILTON A. GILBERT
MONROE GOLDWATER
MILTON A. GORDON
HARRY E. GOULD
ARNOLD M. GRANT
MATTHEW GUINAN
SAM HARRIS
STANLEY J. HARTE
CRANE HAUSSAMEN
MORRIS IUSHEWITZ
AARON L. JACOBY
MRS. ROBERT KINTNER
MRS. ALBERT D. LASKER
FRANCIS S. LEVIEN
WILLIAM H. McKEON
GERARD OESTREICHER
MRS. C. MICHAEL PAUL
LILLIAN L. POSES
WILLIAM POSNER
JACOB POTOFSKY
ALEX ROSE
VINCENT SARDI, JR.
REV. GARDNER C. TAYLOR
EDWIN A. TENNANT, JR.
HARRY VAN ARSDALE
THOMAS J. WATSON
Vice Chairmen

AUSPICES
Democratic National Committee
Democratic State Committee
Citizens for Kennedy

COMMITTEE AND PATRONS

John Q. Adams
Victor L. Anfuso
Ruth H. Axe
Jean P. J. Baltzell
Francis J. Barry
Benjamin Botwinick
Seymour Boyers
Mrs. Louis Broido
Walter Brotherton
Charles Buchannan
Charles Buckley
Hugh L. Carey
Milton M. Carrow
John H. Cassell
Michael Castaldi
Vincent A. Catoggio
Emanuel Celler
Lansdell K. Christie
John Clancy
Sidney Cohn
John T. Collins
Robert E. Condon
William J. Connellan
Edward N. Costikyan
Edouard Cournand
Stephen R. Currier
Mrs. Tobe Coller Davis
Thomas J. Deegan, Jr.
Jack deSimone
Robert Doherty
John W. Dolan
F. Roger Downey
John F. English
John H. Farrell
Abraham Feinberg
George Feldman
Frank D. Fernandez
Jerry Finkelstein
Leon J. Finley
Henry J. Fischbach
Daniel Flanagan
Richard M. Flynn
Elennor Clark French
Henry Garfinkle
Mrs. Louis S. Gimbel, Jr.
W. R. Grace
Mrs. William Greenburg
Jennie Grossinger
Randolph Guggenheimer
Mae Gurevich
W. Averell Harriman
Mrs. Crane Haussamen
Leland Hayward
David M. Heyman
Donald Hoffman
John Hogan
Louis Hollander
Tom Hughes
Sol Hurok
George Hyam
Alfred P. Ilch
William Jaffe
Eric Johnston
J. Raymond Jones
Nathan I. Kalikow
Allan H. Kalmus
Jacob M. Kaplan
Frank E. Karelsen
Fred Katz
Mrs. Edna F. Kelly
Eugene J. Keogh
C. D. King
Philip Klutznick
Mrs. Henry Goddard Leach
Emmett J. Leahy
Evelyn S. Lehman
Orin Lehman
Alan Jay Lerner
Nathan W. Levin
Arthur Levitt
Samuel B. Lewis
Harold F. Linder
Robert A. Lindsay
Louis A. Lotito
Edward V. Loughlin
Joseph Love
Charles Luckman
William F. Luddy
John J. Lynch
Thomas P. Lynch
Angelo J. Martone
Steven Masters
William J. McGawon
Richard C. Miles
Robert Millonzi
Frank Montero
George Moore
Abraham J. Multer
Dr. Godfrey Nurse
James O'Connell
Raymond O'Connell
John O'Donnell
Paul O'Dwyer
John O'Rourke
Frank Pace, Jr.
Arnold M. Picker
Jack I. Poses
Charles F. Preusse
William Reilly
Irving Riese
Murray Riese
Meshulam Riklis
Herman Robbins
John E. Roe
C. Edward Rowe
Samuel Rubin
Jack Rudin
Lewis Rudin
Samuel Rudin
David V. Russell
Ralph E. Samuel
Howard Samuels
Dore Schary
Mrs. David A. Schulte, Sr.
David A. Schulte, Jr.
Norman Seidenwurm
Milton Shalleck
Max L. Shulman
Ed Sitpel
William A. Shea
Martin H. Sher
J. Meyer Shine
John J. Shubert
Maury Silberstein
Robert E. Simon, Jr.
Herbert M. Singer
C. R. Smith
Francis J. Souhan
Harvey M. Spear
Roger L. Stevens
Mrs. Maurice Stone
Nathan Strauss III
James A. Taylor, Jr.
Maurice Templesman
Clifton Toll
Mrs. Ronald Tree
Morris Uchitel
William vanden Heuvel
Arthur K. Watson
Harry Waxman
Sydney W. Waxman
Morris Weinberg
Irwin Weiner
Joe Weinstein
Edwin L. Weisl
Ted B. Westfall
Ben Wetzler
Lloyd G. Whitebrook
Thomas R. Wilcox
Erwin S. Wolfson
Max Youngstein
Bill Zeck
Victor D. Ziminsky
Herman Zipser

ROSE MARIE DILLER
Finance Director

BLANCHE GOTTLIEB
Associate Director

New York's Birthday Salute to President Kennedy

Produced by Richard Adler

STAR SPANGLED BANNER—Sung by ROBERT MERRILL
Conducted by Paul Taubman

BIRTHDAY OVERTURE
Arranged by Sid Ramin

JACK BENNY

ELLA FITZGERALD
Accompanied by Paul Smith Trio; Paul Smith, piano;
Stan Levey, drums; Wilfred Middlebrooks, bass.

JEROME ROBBINS BALLETS: U. S. A.
Presents excerpts from
"New York Export, Opus Jazz"
Music by Robert Prince; Choreographed by Jerome Robbins

DANNY KAYE
Piano Accompaniment—Sammy Prager; Drums, Russ Patrick
Orchestra Conducted by Sidney Kaye; Johnny Mann Singers

PRESENTATION OF COLORS BY THE ARMED FORCES

HENRY FONDA

MARIA CALLAS
Accompanist—Charles Wilson

ELLIOTT REID

PEGGY LEE
Accompanied by Benny Carter, conductor, Lou Levy, piano;
Max Bennett, bass; Chino Poso, bongos, Howard Collins; guitar; Mel Lewis, drums.

PETER LAWFORD

MARILYN MONROE

JIMMY DURANTE and EDDIE JACKSON

BOBBY DARIN
Accompanied by Bobby Scott, piano; Ronnie Zito, drums;
Milton Norman, guitar; Richard Behrke, conductor.

HENRY FONDA

MIKE NICHOLS and ELAINE MAY

DIAHANN CARROLL
Orchestra Conducted by Peter Matz

FINALE
Excerpts from the American Musical Theater—(1940-1960)

Conceived by Richard Adler

Choral Arrangement by Colin D. Romoff

Conducted by Hal Hastings

ROBERT F. WAGNER
Mayor of New York City

JOHN F. KENNEDY
President of the United States

CHORUS

Issa Arnal	Darrell J. Askey
Helen Baisley	Raymond Byrne
Georgia Creighton	Lester Clark, Jr.
Lee Dougherty	Al De Sio
Patricia Finch	Charles Dunn
Iris Hanisch	Jay Gerber
Lee Hooper	Scott Gibson
Maryann Kerrick	Victor R. Helou
Anne Krueger	Lee Howard
Sherry Lambert	Chuck James
Linda North	James Lowe
Mary Roche	Henry Lawrence
Maudeen Sullivan	Robert Sharp
Mimi Vondra	Gordon R. Watkins
Paula Wayne	Arthur Wright
Clark Morgan	

CREDITS

Associate Producer	Earl Blackwell
Talent Coordinator	Jean Dalrymple
Musical Director	Hal Hastings
Lighting By	Sam Leve
Decorations By	Robert Rowe Paddock
Assistant to the Producer	Jerome I. Meyers
Production Stage Manager	Chet O'Brien
Assistant Production Stage Manager	Ira Cirker
Assistant Stage Managers	Keith Holzman James E. Wall
Production Coordinator	Robert M. Ratner
Press Relations	Allan Kalmus Paul Pepe
Production Assistant	Homer Poupart

Printed by The Georgian Lithographers, Inc.

President Kennedy's Birthday Party

MAY 19, 1962

MADISON SQUARE GARDEN

GALA ALL STAR SHOW

ORCHESTRA

SEC. E ROW 11 SEAT 4

CONTRIBUTION $100. PER PERSON

New York's Birthday Salute To The President, Inc.

SPONSORED BY THE STATE AND NATIONAL DEMOCRATIC COMMITTEES AND CITIZENS FOR KENNEDY

This ticket may not be sold or offered for sale at a premium or otherwise. This endorsement is made in conformity with the General Business Law of the State of N.Y.

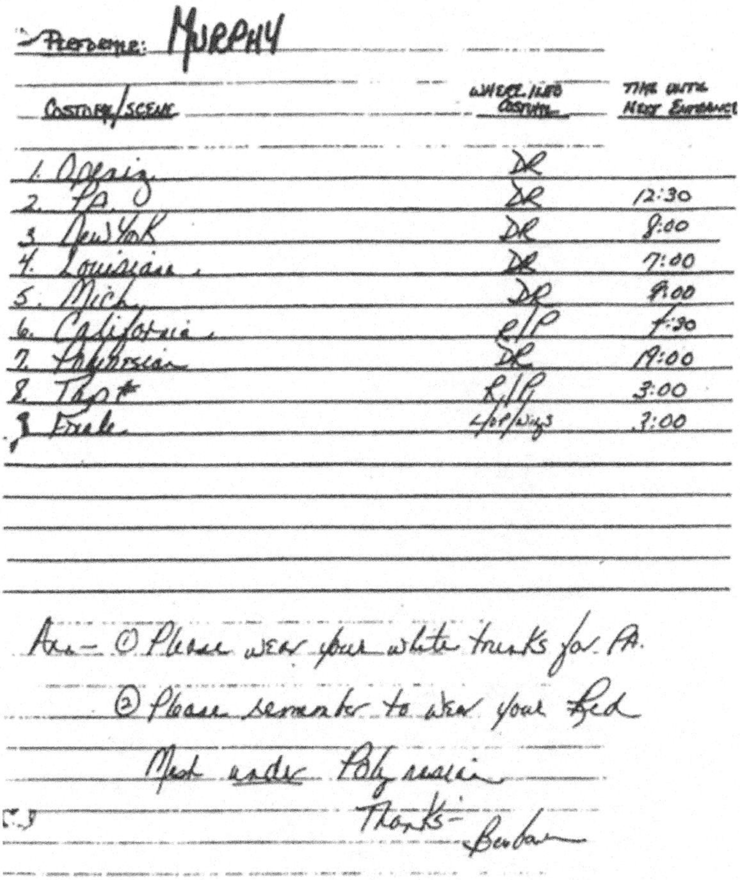

Performer: MURPHY

Costume/Scene	Where Into Costume	Time Until Next Entrance
1. Opening	DR	
2. PA.	DR	12:30
3. New York	DR	8:00
4. Louisiana	DR	7:00
5. Mich.	DR	9:00
6. California	R/P	4:30
7. [illegible]	DR	19:00
8. Tap*	R/P	3:00
9. Finale	L/P/Wigs	3:00

Ann — ① Please wear your white trunks for PA.

② Please remember to wear your Red Mesh under Poly [illegible]

Thanks — Barbara

THESE NOTES ARE FROM WARDROBE FOR ME.
THIS THE "AMERICA" SHOW WAS MY FINAL SHOW FOR RADIO CITY MUSIC HALL.
WHEN ONE HAD AN ENTRANCE ON PROMPT AND/OR AN EXIT OR ANOTHER ENTRANCE ON STAGE LEFT, THAT WAS LITERALLY LIKE WALKING A CITY BLOCK AS PROMPT WAS ON 51st STREET AND OP WAS ON 50th STREET.

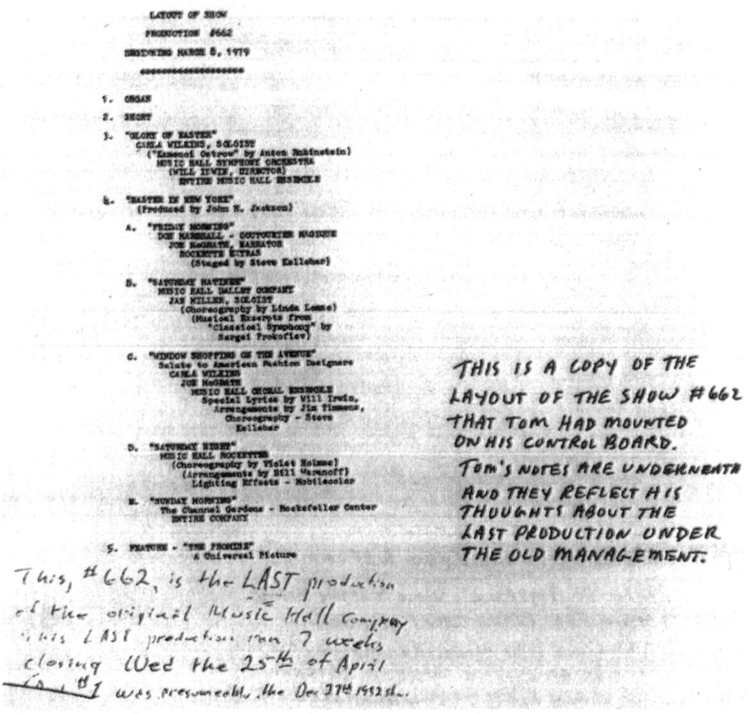

LAYOUT OF SHOW

PRODUCTION #662

BEGINNING MARCH 8, 1979

1. ORGAN
2. SHORT
3. "GLORY OF EASTER"
   CARLA WILKINS, SOLOIST
   ("Kamenoi Ostrow" by Anton Rubinstein)
   MUSIC HALL SYMPHONY ORCHESTRA
   (WILL IRWIN, DIRECTOR)
   ENTIRE MUSIC HALL ENSEMBLE
4. "EASTER IN NEW YORK"
   (Produced by John H. Jackson)

   A. "FRIDAY MORNING"
   DON MARSHALL - COUTOURIER MAGIQUE
   JOE McGRATH, NARRATOR
   ROCKETTE EXTRAS
   (Staged by Steve Kelleher)

   B. "SATURDAY MATINEE"
   MUSIC HALL BALLET COMPANY
   JAN MILLER, SOLOIST
   (Choreography by Linda Lemme)
   (Musical Excerpts from "Classical Symphony" by Sergei Prokofiev)

   C. "WINDOW SHOPPING ON THE AVENUE"
   Salute to American Fashion Designers
   CARLA WILKINS
   JOE McGRATH
   MUSIC HALL CHORAL ENSEMBLE
   Special Lyrics by Will Irwin,
   Arrangements by Jim Timmens,
   Choreography - Steve Kelleher

   D. "SATURDAY NIGHT"
   MUSIC HALL ROCKETTES
   (Choreography by Violet Holmes)
   (Arrangements by Bill Waranoff)
   Lighting Effects - Mobilecolor

   E. "SUNDAY MORNING"
   The Channel Gardens - Rockefeller Center
   ENTIRE COMPANY

5. FEATURE - "THE PROMISE"
   A Universal Picture

This, #662, is the LAST production
of the original Music Hall company
this LAST production ran 7 weeks
closing Wed the 25th of April
[illegible] #1 was presumeably the Dec 27th 1932 sh…

THIS IS A COPY OF THE
LAYOUT OF THE SHOW #662
THAT TOM HAD MOUNTED
ON HIS CONTROL BOARD.
TOM'S NOTES ARE UNDERNEATH
AND THEY REFLECT HIS
THOUGHTS ABOUT THE
LAST PRODUCTION UNDER
THE OLD MANAGEMENT.

The Living Nativity was the final glorious presentation of the Christmas Show. A cast of humans and animals endeavored to convey a pageant that had originated with St. Francis of Assisi in 1223 in Graccia, Italy. St. Francis believed the spirit of Christmas could be kept alive by presenting a realistic portrayal of the Nativity. The reading of "One Solitary Life" by an unknown writer is one of the most poignant parts of the entire pageant.

Even though it was toward the end of the run, I had written in my journal on December 30, 1980. "Wooden Soldiers fall hit hard and crooked tonight - wrenched back; Susan and Dot fell hard out of line." The wooden Soldier fall was capricious. Sometimes the fall would be too slow, sometimes it would be too fast. Often there was a lot of blame to go around, but I know of no one who got seriously hurt doing that fall.

On January 6 of the New Year, we began rehearsals for the Peter Allen show. Three days later we finished the soft shoe number to "Everything Old Is New Again." We also took time that day to shoot some publicity photos for Mainliner Magazine for United Airlines. Both Bob Jani and Dick Evans, Executive Vice President and Chief Operating Officer, posed with us. We did 80 kicks to get a good shot.

Though I said it earlier, it's worth repeating that Peter Allen was not only a delightful entertainer, but a delight to work with, also. His choreographer, Christopher Chadman, however, was a task master. I had written in my journal on January 10th that "Chris cleaned up the soft shoe and Rio number right down to the pinkie finger, adding style. When we got a five minute break, it was five minutes exactly. Worked right up until 5:00 p.m." We had begun rehearsals at 10:00 a.m.

On the Thursday, January 15th glamorous opening night of The Peter Allen Show, I had written: "The show started about ten minutes late - Full house. Peter was great. The audience went wild - standing ovation for our soft shoe numbers with Peter. What a fabulous evening. Everyone was a nervous wreck all evening, but the show went beautifully. Audience tore the house down. The camel did great, too."

On the second day of the show, a film crew taped it for Cable TV. Mayor Koch and Carol Lawrence were in the audience. The audience was still responsive as ever. Chris gave us a pep talk tonight and said "Watch out- you're more relaxed tonight. You haven't been rehearsing all day, so your muscles aren't tuned." Being a Bob Fosse disciple, Chris emphasized every little gesture, including that pinkie finger. Chris had choreographic words of wisdom, telling us, "My boss Bob Fosse said, 'If you're going to steal, steal from the best.'"

The third time around for the Peter Allen Show they decided to bring it back for a return engagement February 13th and 14th. A packed house, the audience went wild again with thunderous applause and standing ovations. It's worth repeating that Peter Allen was a firecracker of an entertainer–smashing, sensational, spectacular, super and special.

On the 6th of March, we previewed what was to be my final production at Radio City Music Hall-the "America" show. We paid tribute to and sang and danced about every state in the Union--all fifty of them.

For the Hawaiian segment, Violet had gone to an authentic Tahitian dance teacher so she could show us some great hip-swiveling moves. One of the hip movements was like a sideways figure-8, or like the symbol for infinity. The hip movement goes downstage right, upstage right, downstage left, upstage left. One song written for the show was "The Spirit of America" with words and music by Tom Bahler and Mark Vieha. Every state had its own particular song.

Tom and I made the decision to move to California, and I would be leaving in early June. However, there was one more extra-curricular production before our departure: the filming of the movie "Annie" for Columbia Pictures, with John Houston directing. This is from my journal of May 4, 1980:

Rehearsal ANNIE - 9:00 a.m. Went down on stage in rehearsal clothes for finale rehearsal. The arches were in different positions, but no one in charge seemed to care, i.e. as far as our spacing was concerned. Sometime after 10:00 a.m. we were excused to go to makeup. Sally, our liaison girl, had us rendezvous with her in the hall at noon, in full costume and makeup. But we didn't go at noon. We waited around in costume, and at 1:00 p.m. we were excused for lunch. Back upstairs, did more sitting around. Finally went down after a half-hour rehearsal in the large hall from 5:30 to 6:00 p.m. At 7:00 p.m. the first assistant director said, "There are a bunch of ladies out there I owe an apology to. This take will be our very last take of the day." So we spent the day getting in and out of costume twice, reapplying makeup and getting nothing in the can. This is the difference between film and theatre. At least, in theatre, one can see something growing; whereas in film there's an awful lot of sitting around and waiting.

May 5, 1980–8:00 a.m. call for makeup. 9:00 a.m. on stage - in costume.

Our finale was completely changed; spent the morning rehearsing and restaging. They finally started to shoot after noon. At 1:25 p.m. first accident on the set; a girl had fallen and hurt her ankle, so the first Asst. Director broke for lunch. At 2:25 p.m. rehearsing and shooting resumed, but not necessarily with us. It was a wrap for us at 7:00 p.m.

There were many complex scenes in this film, one of which was a movie within a movie. Daddy Warbucks had bought out a whole house at Radio City Music Hall, and he takes Annie and her dog Sandy to the show. So, the three of them are sitting out in the house. On stage, a film director is shooting a movie. The director is at stage level. On stage-right there is a scene in Nome, Alaska, complete with a snow machine. Center-stage there is a pirate ship in the Caribbean, and on stage-left is a desert scene in the Arabian Sahara. In the Alaskan scene there are Canadian Mounties holding barking Alaskan Huskie dogs on leashes. When the film director gave the direction to start filming, start the wind machines and the snow, the huskies were barking and running. Upon seeing the dogs, Sandy runs up from her seat across the pit elevator (no orchestra is present) to the sleigh dogs. The director yelled "Cut." The second AD yells "Cut". The third AD yells "Cut."

The stagehands had to sweep up the artificial snow and the scene would start all over again. This went on for hours and was one of the reasons that, though we had a 5:00 a.m. call for hair and makeup, we would sit out in the house in our uncomfortable strapless silver lamé costumes, and never get onstage to be filmed. I was worried about that strapless one-piece costume with the low leg lines so it would look like the 1930's or 1940's, but they were extremely tight across the breasts, so there were no wardrobe malfunctions.

Another all day production number was "Let's Go To the Movies" starring as Daddy Warbuck's secretary, the lovely Ann Reinking, a former ballet girl at Radio City. Miss Reinking does a beautiful dance sequence, which segues into our scene. With bows on our silver tap shoes and an ever bigger bow in our tight-fitting cloche hats, some of us were on different levels on a box and on a rotating wheel–a Busby Berkley effect, again in celluloid.

During the rehearsal period one morning, we were onstage in rehearsal clothes, sans makeup. One of the Rockettes, Pam Stacey, overheard one of some other dancers who had been hired to augment the scene, say of the Rockettes, "Gee, they look like a bunch of New Jersey housewives." Pam wanted to know "and what's wrong with a New Jersey housewife?"

One of the ADs got to one of these dancers, reprimanding her and said, "If you do that again, I'm not going to put the camera on you." As we went up to the dressing room in the crowded passenger elevator, Judy Little, pointing to this one and that one, kiddingly said, "I'm not going to put the camera on you, I'm not going to put the camera on you, I'm not going to put the camera on you!"

"Annie" received lukewarm notices form the critics-somewhat of a bum rap, I think. John Houston hadn't done any musicals and during the filming he was very ill. In fact, he was on oxygen. He must have been looking forward to "tomorrow," when the film would wrap. However, there was a great deal of money spent on this movie. Evidently, they hadn't checked the dailies too closely but, if and when they did, they discovered that in the cavernous Music Hall the lighting was too dark. When the film company got back to Los Angeles, they had to hire other dancers to pose as Rockettes and re-film the scenes in a studio. That was a pretty costly lighting mistake since we were all paid Screen Actors Guild rates, which at that time was $900 a week and they had to pay us again since it was in our contract, even though other dancers were in our place.

On Friday, May 22, 1981, my mother came down from Boston to see her dancing daughter perform for the last time on the Music Hall stage. My dad would do the same thing four days later. But my official last day was on June 3rd. Good-bye, or at least so-long, to those eye-high kicks, cramp-roll time steps, holdover rehearsals, prep rehearsals, footlights, stage elevators, the turntable, the 100-foot proscenium, la passarelle (the runway), and the theatre with an orchestra level and three balconies. There was none other like it in the world.

This is my final entry in my journal of my Radio City Music Hall career:

Pam Kelleher, Joan Pier, Phyllis Wujko, Susan Theobald and Susan Boron took me to dinner at Assembly, our local watering hole on 51st Street, just down the street from the stage door. Later, Stephen Kelleher joined us. Assembly was anxious for the table, so we slipped down to Old Times.

When we returned to the dressing room just in time for call, everyone was gathered around my place. What a send-off they gave me: champagne, my Rockette charm and, best of all, the warmest affection. I love these girls, and I can't write anymore now because I'm starting to cry. (I'm starting to cry right now, as I'm rereading and rewriting this.)

I gave a short speech to the girls telling them that I felt strange, that I was moving to the OP side of the country (and I was used to "working prompt"). I added that I realized everyone would be in a hurry to get home after the last show, but if they could just spare a second, I was going to do something I'd wanted to do for a long time. Then I told them, "I'm going to burn my bra." You might remember what I did as a kid at Camp Wabunaki, raising the bra up the flagpole. And now, burning my bra. I guess it's just a bra thing.

The fabulous evening was climaxed by Jorge Camp, Susan Theobald, Tom and I going to Cantina (a Mexican restaurant on the corner of the street where we lived) and running into Elizabeth Taylor and Maureen Stapleton, who were doing "The Little Foxes" on Broadway.

During the last show, unbeknownst to me, Phyllis pinned a sign on the back of my costume that read "California - Here I Come." I guess since the show was all about America and the states in it, the stage manager let me go on with the sign on my back. Often in shows, cast members will do little things to entertain other cast members on stage unbeknownst to the audience.

The contour curtain came down on my final show and, back up in the dressing room I had the strangest feeling looking at my place, my locker, and my costumes that the costume department had had to reconstruct (they always had to do something to my bras indifferent shapes and designs, depending on the design of the costume), and over to the sink we went. I set the bra on fire. I burned my bra, though I had mixed emotions about it.

Yes, it was a feeling of liberation, but also was of trepidation. Where was I going? And what was I going to do when I got there? Was this the final finale? Were the footlights and spotlights going to dim now forever? That was a scary feeling.

After the finale of "Come Follow The Band." in which we all wore red, white and blue costumes and carried drums that we beat with drumsticks, the contour curtain came down and separated me from the orchestra and three balconies for the last time. When again, if ever again, would I look out and smile out to an audience and receive that marvelous thank you in response–APPLAUSE!

Backstage romances were certainly cultivated at Radio City. I guess I came to realize what a truly great friend Tom was the night of the 1965 blackout. (No, we were not stuck in an elevator, which was perhaps too bad since that is the night I made my horrific New York singing debut. Today I'd be booted off American Idol pronto!) Tom sent me a very long telegram telling me that I had gone on beyond the call of duty. I was hysterical and had gone to my voice teacher Reba Jury crying and so embarrassed and angry with myself. I had always had a fear of singing in public; not speaking or dancing, just singing. It all goes back to that terrible singing debut at E.J. Harrington School in Lynn, Massachusetts when I was in second grade. That had been a disaster, too. I knew it at age seven, and I knew it at twenty-four. But Tom soothed my wounds and was compassionate, understanding and encouraging.

With four, and at holidays five shows a day, Radio City Music Hall had a winning formula for 40 years. Each stage show's length was dependent on the length of the currently running feature film. If the movie ran long, the stage show would be shorter; if the movie was short, the stage show would be longer. In all it would add up to about three hours worth of entertainment.

With shorter films it was difficult to get things done between shows, especially if you wanted to go home and prepare dinner. When Tom and I raced home, I would take no longer than 15 minutes to get dinner on the table. I'd prepare everything I could in the morning–a salad (minus the dressing) and whatever I could pre-cook. Looking back on it, I don't know how we did it with just fifteen minutes to prepare, fifteen minutes to eat, and fifteen minutes to exit. It was truly eat- and-run.

One day we had gone to a restaurant on Fifth Avenue called Patricia Murphy's, and our waiter took so long to bring the check that we had to run out of the restaurant without paying. We did go back and pay our bill later, but "the show must go on." In fact, time was of such essence that one time I asked Tom to call the Assembly restaurant, just down the street from the 51st Street stage door, and ask them put two swordfish on the grill. Tom's boss John Lemac kidded Tom saying, "What do you do, call your order in ahead of time now?"

EPILOGUE

BE CAREFUL COMING ON STAGE, PLEASE NUMBER ONE ELEVATOR IS DOWN

It is truly amazing that more accidents didn't happen over the years. There was always such a rush to get that show opened on time. With so much to do and so little time to do it, it is a testament to the skill and craftsmanship of the stage crew that more mishaps did not occur over the decades. This was especially true before 1979, when we would end one production on a Wednesday and on Thursday, always on schedule, open with a new production. Looking back on it, I don't know how we did it. Sheer will power, lots of rehearsals, and lack of sleep in order to ascertain the show must go on.

Of course, along with exhaustion came nerves of steel or, at the very least, nervous energy. Those nerves were put into overtime when we did extra, on-the-side shows such as Macy's Thanksgiving Day Parade, various television shows, including one other very exciting live show–Saturday Night Live with Howard Cosell. Our legs were trembling in our tights when we heard the TV stage manager shout, "10-9-8-7-6-5-4-3-2-1, CAMERA!"

With the nerves and terror came gratification, satisfaction and the feeling of pleasing an audience. Dancing itself was sheer joy, made especially joyous by the glory of dancing to a wonderful live orchestra. When we'd return from a time-off week, it seemed that our legs would fly as we warmed up in the wings. Careful attention had to be paid to new girls entering the line for the first time. A new girl might have a tendency to, inadvertently, pull at a waist or push at a back when it was imperative for each girl to place her hand gently in the middle of the other girl's back, just beneath her bra, while the girl on the other side would have her hand below the other hand. It was right-over-left. In other words, it should be just as she were kicking by herself and not hanging onto the girls on either side.

The years have kicked by to a real fast tempo, but many former Rockettes had stayed in touch. In fact, there is a Rockette Alumnae Association, which meets regularly. As of this writing, Patty DeCarlo Grantham is now president of the organization. Some of the alumnae, now grandmothers, are still teaching dance and even perform when we have a gala celebration, a time when we raise funds for charity. Recently we were visited by a former Rockette, Louise Neistat, who is now 89 years old and still teaching dance at her studio in Connecticut. She cautioned us that "If you dance, don't stop, because if you do, your body will just curl up." Words of wisdom from a former Rockette who danced on the Great Stage from 1941 to 1943. She danced behind those footlights the year I was born. Maybe she danced on my line-up spot.

So, for the senior set, "When you wake up in the morning and your arabesque is low, do your plié." We used to sing this in the dressing room to the tune of "Pretty Baby."

"When you wake up in the morning and your arabesque is low, do your plié. Do your plié.

Now, go onto arabesque, glissade and then assemblé, but do your plié. Do your plié.

Pas de chat and pas de bourré and dé-v-e-lopp-é, but don't forget that old plié.

When you wake up in the morning and your arabesque is low, do your plié. Do your plié!"

Girls have to start training very young, but it is not unusual for a young man to start training in dance as late as his teens, or even early twenties and go on to have a career in dance. There are two quotes that I remember fondly. One is from Billy Stevens, a high school classmate I dated. He studied dance and was also on the Lynn English High School football team. Billy told me "I was a better athlete because I was a dancer; I wasn't a better dancer because I was an athlete." Romayne Strilka Switch, a dancer's dancer who worked the end of the Rockette line before I did, said she thought that "Every girl should have the opportunity to make her body as beautiful as possible and ballet is the best way to do it." I have always thought that ballet is to dance as Latin is to language.

So, for every little pixie, pigtail, or ponytail who ever tapped her foot in a dance school, listen to the beat of your heart and your feet, and follow your body's rhythm and plié, plié, plié, and flat, slap and tap, and don't forget those cramp roll time steps. Follow your dreams. I know it's a cliché, but damn it, follow them and remember to aim high and kick high–EYE-HIGH!

My decision to leave the Rockettes was with very mixed emotions. It would not have been as difficult to leave Radio City had I left when we were doing four shows a day, seven days a week. That was a grind. But when we went to two shows a day, with a six day work week (the theatre was closed on Mondays) and started touring, life became more interesting and exciting. Under the old management at Radio City I danced in 172 productions and in one of those–a Christmas show in the 1960s in which we portrayed angels–there were 105 kicks in our routine. On a five-show day, that's 525 kicks, not including rehearsal kicks and warm-up kicks.

When the new management began in 1979 I danced eight productions plus four tours: the Mini-Tour across the U.S.A. for the New York State Department of Commerce, Lake Tahoe, Las Vegas and London. In those productions there were four or five routines in each of the two shows per day, the matinee and evening performance. Math has never been my forte, but if one adds it up it's a tremendous amount of eye-high kicks including rehearsals, warm-ups and kicks during various shows we did outside the Music Hall, such as the Macy's Thanksgiving Day Parade, The "Rainbow of Stars" show, The Mary Martin Spends Easter at Radio City Music Hall" show, the "Rockette: A Holiday Tribute to Radio City Music Hall," starring Ann Margaret and Gregory Peck, "a Saturday Night Live Show with Howard Cosell, "The Peter Allen Show," and "Annie," it would amount to hundreds of thousands of kicks.

And that, dear reader, is How I Got My Kicks!

The End

ACKNOWLEDGEMENTS

First, I should like to thank Lou Ruggiero, a wonderful actor and a wonderful boyfriend, for giving me not only the encouragement, but my Apple laptop, my brother, William J. Murphy, Jr., the history teacher, who as our dad used to say, "He knows more about World War II than I do and I was in it," and to my parents William Joseph Murphy and Eleanor Beth Stevens Murphy, for sending me to dancing school. A thank you to Sono Osato, former ballet soloist with Ballet Russe de Monte Carlo and American Ballet Theatre, whose encouragement and cautionary advice was "Don't let anything interfere with your book." Special thanks goes to author Rosemary Rennon, my typist, who had to decipher my handwriting and dance terminology, to Jennifer Russo, whose expertise and talent on the computer are a joy to behold, to Career Transition For Dancers, an admirable organization that is so helpful to so many dancers throughout the transition process, and to Alexander Dubé the Executive Director of CTFD, who insures that everything dances along smoothly within CTFD, and to two stellar career counselors at CTFD, Lauren Gordon and Anita Lands, and to CTFD member and former Broadway show dancer, Susan Sigrist. A thank you also goes to author Carol Franz for her professional advice and to author Dr. Michael Salamon for his expert advice. To my proofreaders Helene Hopper, Margo Mayor, JoanAnn O'Rourke, and Patrick O'Rourke, John Sullivan, and Carol Toman Paracat, thank you. Thank you to my neighbors, who had to jump over a fence to help me with my computer, Gina Bellantuono and Salvadore Capozzi.To all my teachers at Apple Computer,

Anthony, Jamie, Marcie, David, Danny, Richard, Yvette, Ryan, John, Mike, Jess, DJ, Richard, Amanda, James, Richie, Alicia, Mike S., Ryan P. Tom, Pete, Leslie, and any I have missed, YOU ARE FANTASTIC. Last, but not least, to THE RADIO CITY MUSIC HALL ROCKETTES and THE ROCKETTE ALUMNAE ASSOCIATION,—thank you for a million kicks and a million laughs. And, to you, dear readers, thank you for reading my book. I'll log off now and shut down the computer. It's time to do a few kicks.

GLOSSARY

Radio City Music Hall Productions
from September 1959–April 1979

Production#	Date, Title, Producer, Rockette routine, Film & cast
494	9/24/59 "Happy Land" (Isralei Show), Producer: Leon Leonidoff, Rockette Routine: Israeli Army soldiers dancing to Kalaniot "Song of the Red Poppy" featuring Shoshana Damari, Skip Martin. Film: "The FBI Story" starring James Stewart and Vera Miles.
495	10/22/59 "Fall Frolic" Producer: Russell Markert, Rockette routine: "Scarecrows" Film: " A Summer Place" starring Richard Egan, Dorothy McGuire, Sandra Dee and Troy Donahue.
496	11/12/59 "Contrasts In Rhythm" Producer: Russell Market, Rockette routine: "The Great March" Film: "The Miracle" starring Carroll Baker and Roger Moore.
497	12/03/59 "The Nativity" & "Yule Moon" Producer: Leon Leonidoff. . . Rockette routine "Rockettes To The Moon" Film: "Operation Petticoat" starring Cary Grant, Tony Curtis and Dina Merrill.

498 1/21/06 "Let's Go Places" Producer: Russell Markert, Rockette routine: "Palm Island." Film: "Never So Few" starring Frank Sinatra, Gina Lollobrigida, Peter Lawford and Steve McQueen.

499 2/11/60 "Far East to Far West" Producer: Russell Markert, Rockette routine: "Prairie Town USA" (cowboy routine) Film: "Once More With Feeling" starring. Yul Brynner and Kay Kendall. .

500 3/3/60 "Music Box Parade" Producer: Russell Markert. . ., Rockette routine: "Orange and Gold Rhythm." Film: " Home From the Hill" starring Robert Mitchum, Eleanor Parker, George Hamilton and George Peppard.

501 3/31/60 "Tulip Time in Holland" Producer: Leon Leonidoff, Rockette routine: "Dutch Number." Film: "Please Don't Eat the Daisies" starring Doris Day and David Niven.

502 5/19/60 "Follies of 1960" featuring Annette Funicello and Dick Roman. Producer: Leon Leonidoff, Rockette routine: "Blossom Time" - Bridesmaids. Film: "Pollyanna" starring Hayley Mills, Jane Wyman and Richard Egan.

503 6/30/60 "Hawaii, USA" Producer: Leon Leonidoff, Rockette routine: "Ship's Belles" - Sailor number. Film: "Bells Are Ringing" starring Judy Holliday and Dean Martin.

504 8/11/60 "Festival" Producer: Russell Markert, Rockette routine: "Beauty And

The Beat." Film: "Song Without End" starring Dirk Bogard and Capucine.

505 9/22/60 "Kol Nidrei" "Three Cheers" Producer: Russell Markert, Rockette routine: "Kicking Up A Storm." Film: "Dark At the Top of the Stairs" starring Audrey Hepburn, Robert Preston and Dorothy McGuire.

506 10/13/60 "Brazil" Producer: Leon Leonidoff, Rockette routine: "A Tasty Treat From Brazil." Film: "Midnight Lace" starring Doris Day and Rex Harrison.

507 11/10/60 "Town and Country" Producer: Leon Leonidoff, Rockette routine: "A la Carte" - Waiter number. Film: "The World of Susie Wong" starring William Holden and Nancy Kwan.

508 12/8/60 "The Nativity" "Holiday Wishes" Producer: Russell Markert, Rockette routine: "Under the Tree" and The Parade of the Wooden Soldiers. Film: "The Sundowners" starring Deborah Kerr and Robert Mitchum.

509 1/19/61 "Viva Italia" Producer: Leon Leonidoff, Rockette routine: "The Garbaldinis" Film: "Where The Boys Are" starring George Hamilton and Yvette Mimieux.

510 2/16/61 "Lights Up" Producer: Russell Markert, Rockette routine: "Sequined Rhythm." Film: "Cimarron" starring Glenn Ford and Maria Schell.

511 3/16/61 "A Spring Bouquet" Producer: Russell Markert, Rockette routine:

"Spring Chicks" Film: "The Absent Minded Professor" starring Fred MacMurray.

512 5/4/61 "Puerto Rico Holiday" Producer: Leon Leonidoff, Rockette routine: "La Merengue" Film: Parrish" starring Troy Donahue, Claudette Colbert and Karl Malden.

513 6/1/61 "Colorama" Producer: Leon Leonidoff, Rocketteca routine: "Fresh Paint" Film: "The Pleasure of His Company" starring Fred Astaire and Debbie Reynolds.

514 7/6/61 "Festival Time" Producer: Leon Leonidoff, Rockette routine" "Playing the Field" Film: "Fanny" starring Leslie Caron, Maurice Chevalier, Charles Boyer and Horst Buchholz.

515 9/7/61 "Kol Nedrei" "Ode To Music" Producer: Russell Markert, Rockette routine: "Cloud 9" Film: "Come September" starring Rock Hudson, Gina Lollabrigida, Sandra Dee and Bobby Darin.

516 10/5/61 "Wings of Glory" Producer: Leon Leonidoff, Rockette routine: Flight Deck" Film: "Breakfast at Tiffany's" starring Audrey Hepburn and George Peppard.

517 11/9/61 "Moonlight and Rhythm" Producer: Russell Markert, Rockette routine: "Rhythm of Dancing" Film: "Flower Drum Song" starring Nancy Kwan, James Shigeta and Myoshi Umeki.

518 12/14/61 "The Nativity" "Holiday Tidings" Producer: Leon Leonidoff, Rockette routine: "Christmas Greetings" Film: "Babes in Toyland" starring Ray Bolger, Tommy Sands, Annette Funicello and Ed Wynn.

519 1/11/62 "Salut à la France" Producer: Russell Markert, can can routine: "Can-Can Moulin Rouge" Film: ""A Majority of One" starring Rosalind Russell and Alec Guinness.

520 2/8/62 "To The Arts" Producer: Marc Platt, Rockette routine: "Art of Relaxing" Film: :" Lover Come Back" starring Rock Hudson and Doris Day.

521 3/15/62 "Do You Remember" Producer: Russell Markert, Rockette routine: "Rainbow Girls" Film: "Rome Adventure" starring Troy Donahue, Suzanne Pleshette, Angie Dickenson and Rossano Brazzi.

522 4/5/62 "Disneyland USA" Producer: Leon Leonidoff, Rockette routine: "Fantasyland" - Bird number (Choreography by Emilia Sherman) Film: "Moon Pilot" starring Tom Tryon, Brian Keith, Edmond O'Brien and Dany Saval.

523 5/17/62 "Stepping Around" Producer: Russell Markert, Rockette routine: "Stepping Around" Film: "Bon Voyage" starring Fred MacMurray and Jane Wyman.

524 6/14/62 "Summertime" Producer: Leon Leonidoff, Rockette routine: "Ladies Day At West Point" West Point March, Film:

"That Touch of Mink" starring Cary Grant and Doris Day.

525 8/23/62 "Ole" Producer: Leon Leonidoff, Rockette routine: "Farruca" Film: "The Music Man" starring Robert Preston and Shirley Jones.

526 9/27/62 "Kol Nedrei" "Sounds" Producer: Marc Platt, Rockette routine: "Take A Letter" Film: "Gigot" starring Jackie Gleason.

527 11/1/62 "Enchanted Island" Producer: Leon Leonidoff, Rockette routine: "Tropical Heartbeat" Film: "Gypsy" starring Natalie Wood, Rosalind Russell and Karl Malden.

528 12/6/62 "The Nativity" "Happy Holidays" Producer: Leon Leonidoff, Rockette routine: "Holly Belles" Film: "Jumbo" starring Doris Day, Jimmy Durante, Martha Raye and Stephen Boyd.

529 1/17/63 "Curtains Up" Producer: Leon Leonidoff, Rockette routine: "Our Pin Up Girls" Film: "The Days of Wine and Roses" starring Jack Lemmon and Lee Remick.

530 2/14/63 "Carnival" Producer: Russell Markert, Rockette routine: "Gaiety" - Carnival in Venice Film: "To Kill A Mockingbird" starring Gregory Peck.

531 3/14/63 "A Young Man's Fancy" Producer: Marc Platt, Rockette routine: (no title) Film: "A Girl Named Tamiko" starring Laurence Harvey and France Nuyen.

532 4/4/63 "In The Spring" Producer: Leon Leonidoff, Rockette routine: "Rockette Line" Film: "Bye Bye Birdie" starring Ann Margaret, Dick Van Dyke and Janet Leigh.

533 5/16/63 "Colorama" Producer: Russell Markert, Rockette routine: (no title) Film: "Spencer's Mountain" starring Henry Fonda and Maureen O'Hara.

534 6/6/63 "To The Marines" Producer: Leon Leonidoff, Rockette routine: "Birthday Girls" Film: "Come Blow Your Horn" starring Frank Sinatra, Lee J. Cobb and Molly Picon.

535 8/1/63 "Europa" Producer: Leon Leonidoff, Rockette routine: 'Pageantry" Film: "The Thrill of It All" starring Doris Day and James Garner.

536 9/9/63 "Kol Nedrei" "From East To West" Producer: Russell Markert, Rockette routine: "Prairie Town USA" - Cowboy routine, Film: "The VIPs" starring Elizabeth Taylor and Richard Burton.

537 10/24/63 "All Around the Town" Producer: Marc Platt, Rockette routine: "Chic, Smart and Smooth" Film: "Mary, Mary" staring Mervin Le Roy, Debbie Reynolds and Barry Nelson.

538 11/14/63 "High Spirits" Producer: . . ., Rockette routine: "Have A Cigar" Film: "The Wheeler Dealers" starring Lee Remick and Games Garner.

539 12/5/63 "The Nativity" "Cheers" Producer: Leon Leonidoff, Rockette

routine: "Season's Greetings" Film: "Charade" starring Cary Grant and Audrey Hepburn.

540 1/23/64 "Musicana" Producer: Russell Markert, Rockette routine: "And More Girls" Film: "The Prize" starring Paul Newman, Elke Sommer and Edward G. Robinson.

541 2/20/64 "The Good Old Days" Producer: Marc Platt, Rockette routine: "Fanciful Fillies" Film: "Captain Newman, M.D." starring Gregory Peck, Angie Dickinson and Tony Curtis.

542 3/19/64 "Alice in Easterland" Producer: Russell Markert, Rockette routine: "Dancing Flowers" Film: "The World of Henry Orient" starring Peter Sellers, Tippy Walker and Angela Lansbury.

543 4/23/63 "Fantasy and Fun" Producer: Marc Platt, Rockette routine: "Birds of A Feather" Film: "The Pink Panther" starring Peter Sellers, David Niven, Capucine, Robert Wagner and Claudia Cardinale.

544 5/21/64 "Junebeams" Producer: Russell Markert, Rockette routine: "Beauty and the Beat" Film: "The Chalk Garden" starring Deborah Kerr, Hayley Mills and John Mills.

545 7/16/64 "Follies 64" Producer: Leon Leonidoff, Rockette routine: "In Living Color," Ballet Company and Rockette in Ravel's "Bolero" Film: "The Unsinkable Molly Brown" starring Debbie Reynolds, Harve Presnell and Ed Begley.

546 9/24/64 "New York, New York" Producer: Leon Leonidoff, Rockette routine: "Toast of the Town," Ballet company and Rockettes in Gershwin's "Rhapsody In Blue" Film: "Mary Poppins" starring Julie Andrews and Dick Van Dyke.

547 11/12/64 "Autumn Album" Producer: Russell Markert, Rockette routine: "Reflections" Film: "Send Me No Flowers" starring Rock Hudson, Doris Day and Tony Randall.

548 12/10/64 "The Nativity" & "Joy Bells" Producer: Russell Markert, Rockette routine: "Parade of the Wooden Soldiers" Film: Father Goose" starring Cary Grand and Leslie Caron.

549 1/28/65 "Headlines" Producer: Leon Leonidoff, Rockette routine: "Gossip Column" Film: "36 Hours" starring James Garner and Eva Marie Saint.

550 3/6/65 "Free and Fancy" Producer: Mark Platt, Rockette routine: "Cloud 9 Lovelies" Film: "Dear Heart" starring Glenn Ford and Geraldine Page.

551 7/1/65 "Rainbow's End" Producer: Leon Leonidoff, Rockette routine: "Easter Parade" Film: "Operation Crossbow" starring George Peppard and Sophia Loren.

552 5/13/65 "Follies 65" Producer: Leon Leonidoff, Rockette routine: Diamonds for Madame Film: "The Yellow Rolls Royce" starring Rex Harrison, Shirley

MacLaine, Ingrid Bergman, George C. Scott and Omar Sharif.

553 7/15/65 "Reflections" Producer: Leon Leonidoff, Rockette routine: "Sweet and Lovely" Film: "The Sandpiper" starring Elizabeth Taylor and Richard Burton.

554 9/16/65 "Lanterns" Producer: Russell Markert, Rockette routine: "Sweet and Lovely" Film: "The Great Race" starring Tony Curtis, Natalie Wood and Jack Lemmon.

555 11/4/65 "Scrap Book" Producer: Mark Platt, Rockette routine: "Top Drawer" Film: "Never Too Late" starring Paul Ford and Maureen O'Sullivan.

556 12/2/65 "The Nativity" & "Star Bright" Producer: Leon Leonidoff, Rockette routine: "Hello Dollies" Film: "That Darn Cat" starring Hayley Mills and Dean Jones.

557 1/20/66 "Contrast & Rhythm" Producer: Russell Markert, Rockette routine: "The Great March" Film: "Judith" starring Sophia Loren and Peter Finch.

558 2/17/66 "Tahiti" Producer: Leon Leonidoff, Rockette routine: "Going Native" Film: "Inside Daisy Clover" starring Natalie Wood and Robert Redford.

559 3/17/66 "Glory of Easter" & "Hello Spring" Producer: Russell Markert, Rockette routine: "Happy Bunnies" Film: "The Singing Nun" starring Debbie Reynolds, Ricardo Montalban and Greer Garson.

560 5/5/66 "All About Love" Producer: Marc Platt, Rockette routine: "36 Reasons To Fall In Love" Film: "Arabesque" starring Sophia Loren and Gregory Peck.

561 6/9/66 "Summertime" Producer: Leon Leonidoff, Rockette routine: "River Belles" Film: "The Glass Bottom Boat" starring Doris Day, Rod Taylor and Arthur Godfrey.

562 7/14/66 "Flying colors" Producer: Leon Leonidoff, Rockette routine: "Milady's Necklace" Film: "How To Steal a Million" starring Audrey Hepburn and Peter O'Toole.

563 9/22/66 "Kol Nedrei" & "Autumn Album" Producer: Russell Market, Rockette routine: "Manhattan Towers" Film: "Kaleidoscope" starring Warren Beatty and Susannah York.

564 10/13/66 "Golden Days" Producer: Leon Leonidoff, Rockette routine: "The Belles of the Ball" Film: "Any Wednesday" starring Jane Fonda, Jason Robards, Rosemary Murphy and Dean Jones.

565 11/10/66 "The Spice of Life" Producer: Marc Platt, Rockette routine: "Swinging Beat" Film: "Penelope" starring Natalie Wood, Ian Banner and Dick Shawn.

566 12/1/66 "The Nativity" & "Happy Holidays" Producer: Russell Markert, Rockette routine: "Twinkle Tot" Film: "Follow Me, Boys" starring Fred MacMurray and Vera Miles.

567 1/19/67 "Winter Cruise" Producer: Leon Leonidoff, Rockette routine: "Ship's

Belles" Film: "Hotel" starring Rod Taylor, Catherine Spaak and Karl Malden.

568 2/16/67 "Stepping Along" Producer: Russell Markert, Rockette routine: "Fiddle Faddle" Film: "The 25th Hour" starring Anthony Quinn and Virna Lisi.

569 3/9/67 "Spring Tidings" Producer: Leon Leonidoff, Rockette routine: "Spring Cleaning" Film: "How To Succeed In Business Without Really Trying" starring Robert Morse and Michelle Lee.

570 4/27/67 "Hail Canacaczda" Producer: Leon Leonidoff, Rockette routine: "They Always Get Their Man" Film: "Two For The Road" starring Audrey Hepburn and Albert Finney.

571 5/25/67 "Alive And In Color" Producer: Dolores Pallet, Rockette routine: "Dangerous Mission" Film: "Barefoot in the Park" starring Robert Redford and Jane Fonda.

572a 8/17/67 "Jeweled Moments" Producer: Russell Markert, Rockette routine: "Colorama" Film: "Up the Down Staircase" starring Sandy Dennis and Patrick Bedford.

572b (Rockettes and Ballet Company on strike. All-music program.) "Kol Nedrei" & "Fanfare" Film: The Bobo" starring Robert Parrish, Peter Sellers and Britt Ekland.

573 10/14/67 "Kol Nedrei" & "Fanfare" Producer:? Rockette routine "Georgy Girl"

Film: "The Bobo" starring Robert Parrish, Peter Sellers, and Britt Ekland. .

574 10/26/67 "Showtime" Producer: Marc Platt, Rockette routine: "U.F.O" Film: Wait Until Dark" starring Audrey Hepburn, Alan Arkin and Richard Crenna.

575 11/30/67 "The Nativity" & "Cheers" Producer: Leon Leonidoff, Rockette routine: "Jingle Bells" Film: "The Happiest Millionaire" starring Fred MacMurray, Tommy Steele, Greer Garson and Geraldine Page.

576 1/18/68 "Confetti" Producer: Russell Markert, Rockette routine: "Rhythm and Girls" Film: "How To Save Your Marriage and Ruin Your Life" starring Jack Albertson and Dean Martin.

577 2/8/68 "Gala Royale" Producer: Leon Leonidoff, Rockette routine: "Best Foot Forward" Film: " Sweet November" starring Sandy Dennis, Anthony Newley and Theodore Bikel.

578 2/29/68 "Curtains Up" Producer: Marc Platt, Rockette routine: "Top Drawer" Film: The Secret War of Harry Frigg" starring Paul Newman and Sylvia Koscina.

579 3/21/68 "Glory of Easter" & Spring Bouquet" Producer: Russell Markert, Rockette routine: "Spring Chicks" Film: "The One and Only Genuine Original Family Band" starring Walter Brennan, Buddy Ebsen, Leslie Ann Warren and John Davidson.

580 5/2/68 "Words and Music" by Irving Berlin. Producer: Leon Leonidoff, Rockette routine: "Going Hollywood" Film: "The Odd Couple" starring Jack Lemmon and Walter Matthau.

581 8/8/68 "Luau" Producer: Leon Leonidoff, Rockette routine: "Hula Maidens" Film: " Where Were You When the Lights Went Out?" starring Doris Day, Robert Morse, Terry-Thomas and Steve Allen.

582 9/19/68 "Kol Nedrei" & "Joy a Go-Go" Producer: Marc Platt, Rockette routine: "From Head To Toe" Film: "Hot Millions" starring Peter Ustinov, Maggie Smith, Karl Malden and Bob Newhart.

583 10/17/68 "Hooray For Hollywood" Producer: Dolores Pallet, Rockette routine: "Public Enemies" Film: "Bullitt" starring Steve McQueen, Robert Vaughn and Jacqueline Bisset.

584 "The Nativity" & "Joy Bells" Producer: Russell Markert, Rockette routine: "Xmas Cookies" Film: "The Impossible Years" starring David Niven, Lola Albright, Chad Everett and Ozzie Nelson.

585 1/16/69 "Pleasure Bound" Producer: Leon Leonidoff, Rockette routine: "Les Girls" Film: "The Brotherhood": starring Kirk Douglas, Alex Cord, Irene Papas, Luther Adler and Susan Strasberg.

586 2/13/69 "City Rhythms" Producer: Russell Markert, Rockette routine: "Manhattan Towers" Film: "Mayerling"

starring Omar Sharif, Catherine Deneuve, James Mason and Ava Gardner.

587 3/13/69 "Glory of Easter" & "The Spring Thing" Producer: Leon Leonidoff, Rockette routine: "Ambassadors of Spring" Film: "The Love Bug" starring Dean Jones, Michelle Lee and Buddy Hackett.

588 4/24/69 "Fables and Fancies" Producer: Marc Platt, Rockette routine: "Birds of a Feather" Film: "If It's Tuesday, This Must Be Belgium" starring Suzanne Pleshette, Ian McShane and Mildred Natwick.

589 5/22/69 "Daily News" Producer: Leon Leonidoff, Rockette routine: "Center Fold" Film: "Winning" starring Paul Newman, Joanne Woodward, Richard Thomas and Robert Wagner.

590 7/3/69 "Colorama" Producer: ., Rockette routine: "Fiddle Faddle" Film: True Grit" starring John Wayne, Glen Campbell and Kim Darby.

591 8/28/69 "Starshower" Producer: Marc Platt, Rockette routine: "Hot and Cold" Film: "The Gypsy Moths" starring Burt Lancaster, Deborah Kerr and Gene Hackman.

592 9/25/69 "Happenings" Producer: Dolores Pallet, Rockette routine: "Queen of the House" Film" "The Christmas Tree" starring William Holden and Virna Lisi.

593 10/23/69 "Here and There" Producer Russell Markert Rockette routine "Prairie Town USA" Film: "Hail Hero" starring

Michael Douglas, Arthur Kennedy and Teresa Wright.

594 11/13/69 "That's Life" Producer: Marc Platt, Rockette routine: "Chic, Smart and Smooth" Film: "The Brain" starring Anne Heywood and Peter Van Eyck.

595 12/04/69 "The Nativity" & "The Fabulous Year" Producer: Leon Leonidoff, Rockette routine: "Forward Pass" Film: "A Boy Named Charlie Brown" Voices of Peter Robbins and Pamelyn Ferdin. An Animated film.

596 1/22/70 "Stepping Around" Producer: Russell Markert, Rockette routine: "Rhythm and Girls" Film: "Viva Max" starring Peter Ustinov, Pamela Tiffin and Jonathan Winters.

597 2/12/09 "Hail To The Queen" Producer: Leon Leonidoff, Rockette routine: "Fantasia Tropicana" Film: "Tick...Tick...Tick" starring Jim Brown, George Kennedy and Frederic March.

598 3/5/70 "Glory of Easter" & "Potpourri '70" Producer: Leon Leonidoff, Rockette routine: "The Rockettes" Film: "Airport" starring Burt Lancaster, Dean Martin, George Kennedy and Helen Hayes.

599 5/28/70 "Swing to the 70s" Producer: Leon Leonidoff, Rockette routine: "Ambassadors of Good Will" Film: "The Out-of-Towners" starring Jack Lemmon and Sandy Dennis.

600 7/23/70 "Bolero" Producer: Leon Leonidoff, Rockette routine: "The Gay Senoritas" Finale: "Ravel's Bolero" Music

Hall Ballet Company and Rockettes. Film: "Darling Lili" staring Julie Andrews and Rock Hudson.

601 8/24/70 "Autumn in New York" & "Kol Nedrei" (as of 10/1/70) Producer: Leon Leonidoff, Rockette routine: "Fall Fashion" "Sunflower" starring Sophia Loren and Marcello Mastroianni.

602 10/29/70 "Set To Music" Producer: Russell Markert, Rockette routine: "Colorama" Film: "The Private Life of Sherlock Holmes" starring Robert Stephens, Colin Blakely, and Genevieve Page.

603 11/19/70 "The Nativity" & "Cheers!" Producer: Leon Leonidoff, Rockette routine: "The Perfect Thirty Six" Film: Scrooge" starring Albert Finney, Alec Guinness and Edith Evans.

604 1/21/71 "Musicana" Producer: Russell Markert, Rockette routine: "Groovy Girls" Film: "Promise At Dawn" starring Melina Mercouri and Assaf Dayan.

605 2/18/71 "A Southern Medley" Producer: Russell Markert, Rockette routine: "Bayou Rhythm" Film: "Wuthering Heights" starring Anna Calder-Marshall and Timothy Dalton.

606 3/11/71 "Glory of Easter" & "Birth of Spring" Producer: Leon Leonidoff, Rockette routine: "Kicking the Clouds Away" Film: "A New Leaf" starring Walter Matthau and Elaine May.

607 5/13/71 "Red, Hot and Blue" Producer: Leon Leonidoff, Rockette routine: "Seeing Red" "Rhapsody In Blue" by George

Gershwin, the Music Hall Ballet and Rockettes. Film: "Plaza Suite" starring Walter Matthau, Maureen Stapleton, Barbara Harris and Lee Grant.

608 7/1/71 "Town Topics" Producer: Leon Leonidoff, Rockette routine: "Diamonds For Madame" "Rhapsody In Blue" by George Gershwin. The Music Hall Ballet and Rockettes. Film: "Murphy's War" starring Peter O'Toole and Sian Phillips.

609 7/29/71 "Remember?" "Rhapsody In Blue" Producer: Peter Gennaro, Rockette routine: "Lucky Lindy" Film: "The Red Tent" starring Sean Connery, Claudia Cardinale and Peter Finch.

610 9/2/71 "It's In Your Stars" Producer: John Jackson, Rockette routine: "Gemini Twins" Film: "See No Evil" starring Mia Farrow and Robin Bailey.

611 9/30/71 "Fall Preview" Producer: Leon Leonidoff, Rockette routine: "On The Great Stage" Film: "Kotch" starring Walter Matthau and Deborah Winters.

612 10/28/71 "Peter Gennaro Presents" Producer: Peter Gennaro, Rockette routine: "Bye, Bye Blackbird" Film: "The Railway Children" starring Dinah Sheridan and Bernard Cribbins.

613 11/11/71 " The Nativity" & "Sawdust and Spangles" Producer: Leon Leonidoff, Rockette routine: "Brilliant Brigade of Bedazzling Zebras" Film: "Bedknobs and Broomsticks" starring Angela Lansbury, David Tomlinson, Roddy McDowall and Sam Jaffe.

614 1/13/72 "... And The Indians" Producer: Peter Gennaro, Rockette routine: "Cherokee" Film: The Cowboys" starring John Wayne, Roscoe Lee Browne, Bruce Dern and Colleen Dewhurst.

615 2/3/72 "Winter Cruise" Producer: Leon Leonidoff, Rockette routine: "At Your Service" Film: Mary, Queen of Scots" starring Vanessa Redgrave, Glenda Jackson, Patrick McGoohan and Timothy Dalton.

616 3/9/72 "Glory of Easter" & "Springsville" Producer: Leon Leonidoff, Rockette routine: "Ambassadors of Good Will" Film: "What's Up Doc?" starring Barbara Streisand and Ryan O'Neal.

617 5/4/72 "He-er-e's Charlie" Producer: John Henry Jackson, Rockette routine: "Seeing Double" - the Glamorous Tramps, Film: "Play It Again, Sam" starring Woody Allen, Diane Keaton and Tony Roberts.

618 6/1/72 "Black Tie" Producer: Peter Gennaro, Rockette routine: "Precision" Film: "The War Between Men and Woman" starring Jack Lemmon, Barbara Harris and Jason Robards.

619 7/6/72 "Luau 72" Producer: Leon Leonidoff, Rockette routine: "Hawaiian Heat Wave" & "Denizens of the Deep" and "The Undersea Ballet" starring Ron and Joy Holiday, Patsy Kelly & Terry Shepherd - Flying Ballet, Film: "Butterflies Are Free" starring Goldie

Hawn, Edward Albert and Eileen Heckart.

620 8/17/72 "Everybody Tap" Producer: Peter Gennaro, Rockette routine: "Tap Type: A Day At the Office" Film: "The Last of the Red Hot Lovers" starring Alan Arkin and Sally Kellerman.

621 9/21/72 "In One Era, Out The Other" Producer Dolores Pallet Film: "Cancel My Reservation" starring Bob Hope and Eva Marie Saint.

622 11/9/72 "The Nativity" & "Greetings!" Producer: Leon Leonidoff, Rockette routine: "Parade of the Wooden Soldiers" Film: "1776" starring William Daniels, Howard da Silva, Ken Howard and Blythe Danner.

623 2/1/73 "The King" Producer: John Henry Jackson, Rockette routine: "The King and The Queens" Film: "The World's Greatest Athlete" starring John Amos, Jan-Michael Vincent and Tim Conway.

624 2/22/73 "Black Tie" Producer: Peter Gennaro, Rockette routine: "Precision" Film: "Charlotte's Web" starring Iwao Takamoto; voices of Debbie Reynolds, Henry Gibson, Paul Lynde, Agnes Moorehead and Charles Nelson Reilly.

625 3/15/73 "Glory of Easter" & "Springtime, Etc." Producer: Leon Leonidoff, Rockette routine: "Dutch Treats" Film: Tom Sawyer" starring Johnny Whitaker, Celeste Holm, Warren Oats, Jeff East and Jodie Foster.

626 5/17/73 "Fifty Happy Years" Producer: Leon Leonidoff, Rockette routine: "Everybody's Cup of Tea" Film: "Mary Poppins" starring Julie Andrews and Dick Van Dyke.

627 6/28/73 "Viva Mexico" Producer: John Henry Jackson, Rockette routine: "The Fiesta Mexicana Company" Film: "Forty Carats" starring Liv Ullmann, Gene Kelly and Edward Albert.

628 8/9/73 "Cool and Easy" Producer: Peter Gennaro, Rockette routine: "Seascape In Beatle Time" Film: "Night Watch" starring Elizabeth Taylor and Lawrence Harvey.

629 9/27/73 "Kol Nedrei" & "Autumn in New York" Producer: Leon Leonidoff, Rockette routine: "The West Point March" Film: "From the Mixed-Up Files of Mrs. Basil E. Frankweiler" starring Ingrid Bergman, Sally Prager and Johnny Doran.

630 10/18/73 "Feathers and Bows" Producer: Peter Gennaro, Rockette routine: "Cherokee" Film: "The Optimists" starring Peter Sellers and Donna Mullane.

631 11/8/73 "The Nativity" & "World-Wide Christmas" Producer: Leon Leonidoff, Rockette routine: "The Perfect 36" Film: "Robin Hood" starring voices of Brian Bedford, Phil Harris, Monica Evans, Pete Ustinov and Terry Thomas.

632 2/7/74 "Morning, Noon and Evening" Producer: John Henry Jackson, Rockette routine: "Tapping, Typing Secretaries"

Film: "Superdad" starring Bob Crane, Kurt Russell and Barbara Rush.

633 3/7/74 "Glory of Easter" Producer: Leon Leonidoff, & "A Potpourri of Bunnies and Chicks" Producer: Peter Gennaro, featuring the Music Hall Ballet Company as "The Bunnies" and Rockettes as "The Chicks" Film: "Mame" starring Lucille Ball, Robert Preston and Beatrice Arthur.

634 5/16/74 "Say It With Music" Producer: Leon Leonidoff, Rockette routine: "There's No Business Like Show Business" Film: "The Black Windmill" starring Michael Caine, Joseph O'Connor and Donald Pleasence.

635 6/6/74 "Saludo A Columbia" Producer: Leon Leonidoff, Rockette routine: "At the Museo Del Oro" Film: "Herbie Rides Again" starring Helen Hayes, Ken Berry, Stefanie Powers and Keenan Wynn.

636 7/11/74 "New Voices '74" Producer: Peter Gennaro, Rockette routine: "Broadway Rhythms" Film: The Tamarind Seed" starring Julie Andrews, Omar Sharif and Anthony Quayle.

637 8/22/74 "Downbeat, Upbeat" Producer: John Henry Jackson, Rockette routine: "In The Mood" Film: The Girl From Petrovka" starring Goldie Hawn, Hal Holbrook and Anthony Hopkins.

638 11/7/74 "The Nativity" Producer: Leon Leonidoff & "Elves and Belles" Producer: Peter Gennaro, Rockette routine: "Christmas Belles" Film: "The Little

Prince" starring Richard Kiley, Bob Fosse and Gene Wilder.

639 3/6/75 "Glory of Easter" Producer: Leon Leonidoff & "Hare" Producer: Peter Gennaro, Rockette routine: "36 Dancing Girls" Film: "At Long Last Love" starring Burt Reynolds, Cybil Shepherd, Madeline Kahn and Eileen Brennan.

640 4/24/75 "It's In Your Stars" Producer: John Henry Jackson, Rockette routine: "Gemini Twins" Films - An MGM Festival: "Gone With The Wind" starring Clark Gable and Vivien Leigh, and (starting 5/1/75) "2001: A Space Odyssey" starring Kier Dullea, William Sylvester and Gary Lockwood, (starting 5/8/75) "Singin' In The Rain" starring Gene Kelly, Donald O'Connor and Debbie Reynolds, (starting 5/15/75) "Doctor Zhivago" starring Omar Sharif, Julie Christie, Geraldine Chaplin, Alec Guinness, Siobhan McKenna, Ralph Richardson and Rod Steiger.

641 5/22/75 "Prelude '76" Producer: Peter Gennaro, Rockette routine: "The Drum Brigade" Film: "The Wind and the Lion" starring Sean Connery, Candice Bergen, Brian Keith and John Huston.

642 6/26/75 "Let Freedom Ring" Producer: John Henry Jackson, Rockette routine: "Up The Street" Film: "Bite the Bullet" starring Gene Hackman, Candice Bergen and James Coburn.

643 6/31/75 "Star-Spangled Rhythm" Producer: Peter Gennaro, Rockette

routine: "Broadway Rhythms" Film: "Hennessy" starring Rod Steiger and Lee Remick.

644 11/6/75 "Happy Holiday, America" Producer: Peter Gennaro, Rockette routine: "The Glittering Snowflakes" Film: "The Sunshine Boys" starring Walter Matthau and George Burns.

645 (Like The Lost Chord, notes on this production are missing.)

646 5/13/76 "From Bach To Bacharach" Producer: John Henry Jackson, Rockette routine: "All that Jazz" Film: "The Blue Bird" starring Elizabeth Taylor, Todd Lookingland, Patsy Kensit, Jane Fonda and Ava Gardner"

647 6/17/76 "Celebrate '76" Producer: Peter Gennaro, Rockette routine: "Red, White and Blue Rainbow" Film: "Harry and Walter Go to New York" starring James Caan, Elliot Gould, Diane Keaton and Michael Caine.

648 7/29/76 "La Fantaisie Du Cirque" Producer: John Henry Jackson, Rockette routine: "Ponies Parisiennes" Film: "The Swashbuckler" starring Robert Shaw, James Earl Jones, Peter Boyle and Genevieve Bujold.

649 10/7/76 "Gershwin - Classic Jazz" Producer: John Henry Jackson, Rockette routine: "Americans In Paris" Film: "A Matter of Time" starring Liza Minnelli, Ingrid Bergman and Charles Boyer.

650 11/4/76 "The Nativity" & "Snowflakes" Producer: Peter Gennaro, Rockette

routine: "March of the Wooden Soldiers" Film: "The Slipper and The Rose" starring Richard Chamberlain, Gemma Craven and Annette Crosbie.

651 3/3/77 "Glory of Easter" & "Top Hats and Tales" Producer: Peter Gennaro, Rockette routine: "Hands and Hats" Film: "Mr. Billion" starring Terence Hill, Valerie Perrine and Jackie Gleason.

652 4/28/77 "Guinness World Records" Producer: John Henry Jackson, Rockette routine: "The Changing of the Guard" - A salute to Queen Elizabeth's Silver Jubilee; Film: "The Sting" starring Paul Newman, Robert Redford and Robert Shaw.

653 5/19/77 "Girls! Girls! Girls! Producer: Peter Gennaro, Rockette routine: "Les Cowgirls" Film: "Smokey and The Bandit" starring Burt Reynolds, Sally Field and Jackie Gleason.

654 6/30/77 "Salute To N.Y.C." Producer: Peter Gennaro, Rockette routine: "Hard Hats" Film: "MacArthur" starring Gregory Peck and Dan O'Herlihy.

655 11/3/77 "The Nativity" & "Glittering Garlands" Producer: Peter Gennaro, Rockette routine: "Glittering Rockettes" Film: "Pete's Dragon" starring Helen Reddy, Jim Dale, Mickey Rooney, Red Buttons and Shelley Winters.

656 3/2/78 "Glory of Easter" & "Springtime Carousel" Producer: Peter Gennaro, Rockette routine: "Carousel" Film: "Crossed Swords" starring Mark Lester, Oliver Reed, Raquel Welch, George C.

Scott, Rex Harrison, Ernest Borgnine and Charlton Heston.

657 4/27/78 "It's Your Music Hall Stars" Producer: John Henry Jackson, Rockette routine: "The World's Most Gorgeous 'Chimney Sweeps'" Film: "The Sea Gypsies" starring Robert Logan and Heather Rattroy.

658 5/18/78 "Rockettes - and then some" Producer: John Henry Jackson, Rockette routine: "Kicks '78" Film: "Fantasia" produced by Walt Disney.

659 6/22/78 "Chiffons" Producer: John Henry Jackson, Rockette routine: "Girls! Girls! Girls!" Film: "Matilda" starring Elliot Gould and Robert Mitchum.

660 8/30/78 "Bizet and Bizazz" Producer: John Henry Jackson, Rockette routine: "The Mississippi Belles" Film: "The Magic of Lassie" starring James Stewart, Lassie, Mickey Rooney and Alice Faye. (Lassie appeared live onstage with this show, arriving each day by limousine with a Yorkshire terrier bodyguard and a Pinkerton detective.)

661 11/2/78 "The Nativity" & "A Merrie Olde Christmas" Producer: John Henry Jackson, Rockette routine: "Puppet Dolls In the Shop Window" Film: "Caravans" starring Anthony Quinn and Jennifer O'Neill.

662 3/8/79 "Glory of Easter & "Easter In New York" Producer: John Henry Jackson, Rockette routine: "Saturday Night" Film: "The Promise" starring

Kathleen Quinlan and Stephen Collins. The following is from Tom's notes: *Note: # 662 was the last production of the original Music Hall Company. This final production ran 7 weeks, closing Wednesday, the 25th of April. (Production # 1 was, presumably, on December 27th, 1932.)

Made in the USA
Columbia, SC
22 April 2025

57013577R00122